WHY CHARITY?

WHY CHARITY?

The Case for a Third Sector

JAMES DOUGLAS

Sponsored by the Yale Program on Non-Profit Organizations

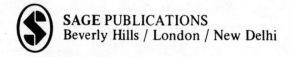

SAGE PUBLICATIONS
Beverly Hills / London / New Delhi

For information address:

SAGE Publications, Inc.
275 South Beverly Drive
Beverly Hills, California 90212

SAGE Publications India Pvt. Ltd.
C-236 Defence Colony
New Delhi 110 024, India

SAGE Publications Ltd
28 Banner Street
London EC1Y 8QE, England

Printed in the United States of America

Library of Congress Cataloging in Publication Data

Main entry under title:

Library of Congress Cataloging in Publication Data

Douglas, James (James A. T.)
Why charity?

Bibliography: p.
1. Charities——Societies, etc. 2. Associations, institution, etc. I. Title.

HV 40.D68 1983 361.7 83-3363
ISBN 0-8039-2003-2

FIRST PRINTING

Contents

WHY CHARITY?

Acknowledgments

I am grateful to Aaron Wildavsky and the Russell Sage Foundation for first stimulating my interest in charitable foundations. During my year at the Russell Sage Foundation I obtained many invaluable insights into the foundations world both from my colleagues there and from the many foundation executives and foundation watchers I was able to meet under the Foundation's aegis. These included the late Emerson Andrews, who was a marvelous repository of lore and anecdotes about the early days of the great foundations.

It was, however, when I spent two years as a Research Associate in the Yale Program on Non-Profit Organizations that I broadened my interest to the Third Sector as a whole and wrote most of this book. I am profoundly grateful to the Yale Program for the opportunity to do this. Under John Simon's direction the Program became a real research community. We exchanged ideas, we commented on each others' papers, and we benefited from a constant stream of visitors to our lunchtime seminars. My debts both to the colleagues in the Program and many of the visitors, they will, I hope, recognize in the text. I feel, however, I must make a special mention of the extraordinary generosity of John Simon, Richard Nelson, and Paul DiMaggio with their time, their knowledge, and their ideas. In thinking about the role of institutions that are neither business nor government, I found myself having to think increasingly about the role and the limitations on government. Here again I must record my indebtedness to another aspect of the Yale Institute for Social and Policy Studies, the regular seminars on political institutions from whose members I obtained much help. I would like to mention in particular Bruce Ackerman, Robert Dahl, James Fishkin, and C. E. Lindblom.

Although my ideas would certainly have been far more superficial but for the help I received from all these, I need hardly say that I alone can be held responsible for the ideas and any remaining idiocies in this text.

—*J. D.*
Evanston, Illinois

1

Introduction

Western civilization has developed two great systems for the allocation of resources. These can conveniently be symbolized by their most distinctive mechanisms: the market and the ballot box. Both have been extensively studied, in both descriptive and normative terms — the market sector of commercial enterprise by economists and the government sector by political scientists and theorists. There are, however, a host of organizations that fit tidily neither into the public, or government, sector nor into the private, or commercial, sector. Why should society need them?

BUSINESS, GOVERNMENT, AND THE THIRD SECTOR

The Filer Commission[1] described these voluntary and philanthropic organizations as the "Third Sector." Known as the Filer Commission, the Commission on Private Philanthropy and Public Needs chaired by Mr. John H. Filer was established in 1973 largely on the initiative of John D. Rockefeller III. The Commission published its own report, *Giv-*

ing in America, and issued, through the Department of the Treasury, some five volumes (amounting to more than 3000 pages) of research papers that constitute the most comprehensive body of scholarly literature available so far about American philanthropy. They gave currency to the idea of distinguishing among three distinct sectors — the "business," the "government," and a "third" sector. This is clearly a good way to start marking out the ground, and it avoids some of the problems raised by other terms. "Voluntary" is confusing when we speak of an institution, such as a university or an opera company, which charges for its services and whose staff are paid. "Nonprofit" is a term that these days could be applied to quite a few commercial establishments. And an organization to protect animals or the natural environment does not necessarily make the love of man its central objective in the way the term "philanthropy" suggests.[2]

The Filer Commission was not primarily motivated by an academic desire to name, define, and classify the structures of contemporary American society. It were established in the aftermath of the Tax Reform Act of 1969 (which many in the world of philanthropy had seen as an attack on the Third Sector). The Act itself was influenced by the hearings of a congressional committee chaired by Representative Wright Patman,[3] during which many criticisms were levied at Third Sector institutions and a few genuine abuses identified. Both to defend the existence of a Third Sector against possible further attacks and to identify what should properly be regarded as abuses of the privileges enjoyed by Third Sector institutions, we need a comprehensive rationale that will enable us to see its place in a free society and to distinguish its proper role from those of the government and commercial sectors.

We know far less about the Third Sector than we do about the other two. We cannot even say with any precision what proportion of national resources is allocated through its agencies as distinct from the agencies of government and commerce. This lack is itself partly a result of the absence of any adequate theoretical framework. As Weisbrod and Long[4] have written, "We cannot define the non-profit sector in a useful manner and we cannot specify what data about it would be of interest. On the other hand, the dearth of theoretical work is to some degree a reflection of the inadequate data with which to test theories."

The Third Sector is not peculiar to the United States. Although a figure cannot be put to it, the volume of resources allocated by nonprofit institutions is significant not only in the United States but in almost every country of Western Europe and probably also in many countries of the Third World. What is perhaps even more important is that the whole shape of European and American society has been profoundly influenced by nonprofit organizations. As Marion Fremont Smith[5] has shown, such organizations far antedate the emergence of the modern commercial enterprise and democratic government as we now understand theses terms. To some extent services we now associate with government or commercial enterprise were originally pioneered by philanthropic institutions. This is clearly true of education and of the welfare services we now associate with a modern state. Not so obvious is the extent to which in earlier times transport, roads, harbors, scholarship, and craftsmanship, much artistic endeavor, health care and hospitals, and even prisons were originally developed by charitable organizations. Quite apart from the quantity of resources distributed without either the compulsion of law or the incentive of profit, the qualitative contribution of the Third Sector has been and remains significant and, as I will argue, distinctive of what we call a free society.

For most of the earlier part of this century, progressive thinkers felt confidence in the power of government to correct the ills of society. In much the same way, somewhat over a century earlier, progressive thinkers had felt confident that wealth, peace, and justice could be attained by liberating the forces of commerce in a free market. The latter position was elaborately articulated by the economists of the classical school — the former somewhat less comprehensively by the politicians of democratic socialism who, in the United States, are by some called "liberals." Our present age lacks confidence in the beneficient power of either governments or markets and seems to be almost equally disillusioned with both. This is perhaps the most compelling of the reasons to readjust our thinking in economics and politics so that adequate attention can be paid to the Third Sector.

There is, admittedly, a lack of rigor about the idea of three sectors. The term "sector" suggests precise boundaries, like those of a political map showing the precise frontiers between nations. Certainly we cannot draw these kinds of boundaries between business, government, and philanthropy. There are publicly owned undertakings that straddle the boundary between business and government. Government has a say in nearly every private undertaking and money in quite a few privately owned businesses. Governments frequently make use of Third Sector institutions as agents to carry out their tasks or as channels for their funds. Third Sector institutions in some cases are almost totally dependent on government funds. Others have used their own funds to embark on new tasks precisely in order to encourage government to take them over. Many commercial, for-profit enterprises have spawned charitable foundations. Others carry out similar philanthropic tasks themselves. Daniel Bell, in *The Coming of Post-Industrial Society,* argues that "what is public and what is private and what is profit and what is not-for-profit is no longer an easy distinction." He quotes, among others, the examples of the aerospace industry, which is (in the United States) private yet dependent on government contracts for some 94 percent of its output; of profitable not-for-profit institutions such as the New York Port Authority and the Triborough Bridge Authority; and of research institutes and universities in which the private institutions are almost indistinguishable from the public institutions. The device of lumping together into a residual category everything that cannot reasonably be considered business or government also includes too much. The family, for example, is neither a business nor a government, but it would be distinctly odd to class it as a form of private philanthropy.

Before one starts to distinguish three sectors of corporate existence, one must distinguish between individuals and their households on the one hand, and organizations with some sort of corporate identity on the other. This distinction is somewhat easier to draw in civil law countries, like France and Germany, than it is in common law countries, like Britain and the United States. Even so, it is not too difficult to distinguish the personal and household sector from what we want to term the Third Sector. More troublesome are those corporate organizations such as, for example, trade unions or political parties, which it is convenient to include in the Third Sector for some purposes but not for others.

The extent to which, in any society, Third Sector organizations are free and healthy is probably as good a measure as any of how far that society can be called free. An absolutely totalitarian society would in theory have nothing but an all-embracing government sector, with government equated with the governing party. In practice, however, even the Soviet system makes use of market mechanisms, notably to control consumption. As systems move toward the ideal of freedom, the separation between the government sector and the Third Sector becomes more marked. Freedom of religion implies the legitimacy of one or more churches distinct from the state and is one of the most basic political freedoms. As we are seeing today in Poland, the demand for freedom is also often reflected in a demand for free trade unions. A system of government that distinguishes its political parties from government to the point that rival political parties compete for office almost meets the definition of democracy as the term is used in the West. Before that stage is reached, however, interest groups and pressure groups distinguishable from government and the ruling party will in most cases have already emerged.

Voluntary associations pursuing the public weal independently of government may arise quite late in the evolution of a free society. Napoleonic France recognized the rights of private property and hence a commercial sector distinct from government, but it was not until quite late in the nineteenth century that the legitimacy of voluntary associations was explicitly recognized. Today the Third Sector in France is as diversified and, in practice, almost as free as it is in any other Western democracy — although the French Third Sector remains somewhat less privileged, notably regarding tax exemption, than is the British or the American. Taking matters to extremes, perhaps a perfectly free society would be entirely organized on the voluntary principle. But that is only to say that perfect freedom can only be achieved by a community of saints.

The Filer Commission did not attempt to define the Third Sector, any more than it tried to define such terms as "voluntary sector" and "private nonprofit sector," which were used as synonyms from time to time. As Daniel Bell suggests, it is probably impossible to give very precise definitions to any of the three sectors. On the other hand, the merit of the term "Third Sector" is that it draws attention to what the organizations constituting it *are not*. It thus encourages us to ask why certain organizations avoid the more usual form of a commercial firm or of a government service.

These two questions — "Why not market?" and "Why not government?" — seem to provide the structure for a rationale or justification for a Third Sector. The theory of market failure (in one or another of its forms) answers the question "Why not market?" An analysis of the political constraints on government should answer the question "Why not government?"

When I first approached this topic, I expected to find a rationale on these lines already worked out.[6] I had long been aware of the theory of market failure as a justification for government intervention in the market, and I had come across references to a concept of government failure analogous to the economic theory of market failure. The idea that these "twin failures" — of the market for private goods and of government constrained by democratic norms — left room for something that is neither government nor commerce was in the air. I was, however, surprised to find that it had never been worked out and that there was no comprehensive body of theory about the place of charity in a free society. There were scattered fragments here and there. There were quite a number of relevant concepts to be found in the law of charities, in welfare economics, in moral philosophy, and in political theory. There was also a fairly extensive literature dealing with the organization and the history of many parts of the Third Sector. These had never been brought together, however, to provide a framework for thinking in a consistent theoretical way about the role and the responsibilities of the Third Sector. It seemed to me that it would be worthwhile bringing together the fragments I could gather from economics and political theory to see what sort of rationale and justification for a Third Sector emerged from these — the disciplines traditionally concerned with the allocation of resources and of roles within society. I was fortunate to be able to pursue this enquiry under the auspices of the Yale Program on Non-Profit Organization, whose guiding spirit, John Simon, was firmly convinced of the need to elaborate a rationale for the Third Sector that might cast light on the role of its institutions and the accountability of their officers.

As I proceeded with this task, I soon became aware of the almost infinite potential ramifications of this approach. Defining the role of the Third Sector by reference to the failures of both governments and markets meant that virtually everything that had anything to do with the economy or the polity would be relevant. I had therefore to impose on myself rather strict, self-denying ordinances, generally in the form of not pursuing any topic too far. The result could only be a preliminary survey and a partial rationale, but I hope that even this very preliminary clearing of the ground may nonetheless prove useful. Even this preliminary and partial rationale does, in fact, challenge some of the conventional wisdom about the role and responsibilities of the institutions within the Third Sector, and I will be entirely satisfied if it persuades others either to challenge my conclusions or to pursue my analysis in greater depth.

OVERVIEW OF THE BOOK

In this book, I report on this search for a Third Sector rationale. Following Chapter 2, in which I seek to define the bases of the three sectors, I recapitulate in summary form, in Chapter 3, the economic notion of market failure. This defines the conditions under which commercial markets can be expected to fail to distribute resources in accordance with what conventional economics postulates will be the way that most closely approximates to the wishes of the society as a whole. In this chapter I am able to draw on a fairly well established body of economic theory. Indeed, it will inevitably seem rather jejune to those already well versed in welfare economics.

A key concept in the theory of market failure is the concept of *externalities* – benefits that spill over into society in such a way that the person providing the benefit cannot be fully recompensed by the benefited parties. This is the traditional argument for government intervention and for the intervention of voluntary nonprofit organizations. It is because no one can be excluded from the benefits of national defense that, from the earliest times, defense has been regarded as the government's responsibility. Hence all citizens are required to contribute to its cost, either through compulsory taxation or compulsory military service or the like. It is because education is believed to benefit not only the people being educated but also the society as a whole that public education is provided by governments, and private educational institutions are granted special legal and tax privileges. This economic concept of externalities seems very similar to the legal concept of public benefit, which has long been recognized as a necessary (but not always sufficient) condition for an activity to be legally classified as charitable. In Chapter 4 I compare the economic and the legal concepts to see how well the notion of externalities fits the range of activities that have traditionally been regarded as charitable.[7]

One weakness in the concept of externalities as a rationale for charity is that it fails to explain an important class of charities, arguably the most perfect: eleemosynary charity, in which those who undertake the activity derive no benefit from it themselves. Not only does the concept of externalities fail to explain the motivation of those who act altruistically in this way; more significantly, it also fails to explain why such an activity should be desirable. Some have tried to get round this difficulty by postulating a desire on the part of the charitable to help others — the charitable prefer the moral satisfactions or "psychic rewards" they get from charitable activity to the benefits they could obtain from other uses of their time or money. I argue that to extend the economic concept of "utility" in this way not only obscures the notion of an externality but actually undermines the very argument that leads to the conclusion that externalities are a market failure. Market failure is not an observed characteristic of markets, but rather, like much of conventional economics, a logical deduction from the basic hypothesis that economic actors will act in such a way as to advance their own material interests. When we see no material benefit accruing to those who provide a service, we assume that the profit motive will provide no incentive for the performance of that service. If the service is needed, we must rely on other incentives, and, therefore, since market forces are not sufficient, we call this "market failure."

The idea that the economy is driven and held together by each individual's thought of his or her own gain is so basic to conventional economics and so challenged by altruistic and idealistic behavior that I devote Chapter 5 to an examination of the limitations of that idea. In this I have been greatly influenced by Albert Hirschman's magisterial study of how the concept of self-interest came to dominate the social sciences.[8] I conclude the chapter with some further criticisms of the market failure rationale, notably its inability to quantify the desirable extent to which market mechanisms need to be supplemented or supplanted by noncommercial activities. This is a theme to which I return in Chapter 8 when discussing Arrow's impossibility theorem.

Before doing so, Chapter 6 discusses a form of the market failure and externalities argument that has been much used in relation to voluntary nonprofit organizations. This is the form that emphasizes the notion of trust which, as Henry Hansmann has pointed out, is closely analogous to the legal concept of a fiduciary relationship.[9] I conclude that, like the generalized forms of the market failure and externalities argument, it is illuminating but fails the rigorous test of providing a definition that is both necessary and sufficient.

Up to this point I have been concerned with the limits of the application of market disciplines as a means of maximizing welfare, and I have been able to draw on a fairly extensive body of analysis and theory. Even, however, if one were able to define perfectly the limits of the market sector, we would still need to distinguish the fields appropriate to each of the two nonprofit forms — the government sector and the Third Sector. Moreover, it is my contention that the limits on the application of governmental authority are even more crucial to the case for a Third Sector than are the limited application of the mechanisms of market exchange transactions. Here I have found a singular paucity of analysis of the theoretical limits on what can be achieved by governmental authority given the constraints of democratic norms. In the next two chapters, 7 and 8, I make a first attempt at analyzing some of these limits. This attempt must be preliminary and inadequate. Clearly there is room for a great deal more conceptual analysis than I can command.

In fact, one economist, Burton Weisbrod,[10] does attempt a theoretical model distinguishing what can be achieved by government from what must be accomplished through voluntary action. This model is, however, cast in the conventional economic terms of demand and supply functions that can be applied to political behavior only with difficulty and does not spring from any essential characteristic of government. What I suggest is that the essential characteristic of government that constrains its role (and is, I suspect, the real prime mover behind Weisbrod's model) is that when government exercises its authority, that authority must be applied universally throughout the jurisdiction. I call this "categorical constraint" and argue that it derives logically from the basic principle of equality before the law. Governments can, of course, define the categories of those to whom a law applies. It can, for example, legislate that all those with a certain level or a certain kind of income shall pay tax at a certain rate, but it cannot allow a taxpayer to opt out, however intensely he or she may dislike or disapprove of the purposes for which the tax is raised. Very occasionally the rigidity of the categorical constraint may be bent somewhat. For example, conscientious objectors may be excused from compulsory military service, but even in that case justice requires some equivalent or greater sacrifice. Weisbrod, in drawing an analogy between the taxpayer paying for the maintenance of a certain level of public service and the customer buying the analogous service, obscures the real nature of the constraint on government, which has more to do with the extent to which the requirements of government are acceptable or tolerable than with the finely graduated degree and direction of individual wants to which a market system can react.

Within its limitations, the market system is an extraordinarily subtle and sophisticated mechanism for making the activities of a society conform to the wants of the individual members of that society insofar as they can be expressed in the language of costs and prices. The ballot box — using that term as shorthand for what is in fact a considerably more complex set of mechanisms — is much cruder. The market routinely aggregates individual preferences. It finds the point of equilibrium between all the choices of all of us both in our roles as consumers and in our roles as producers — and, of course, all of us are both consumers and producers of one or more of the factors of production. It does this responding only to our own free choices — that is to say, the tradeoffs inherent in any economic transaction as we perceive them ourselves. The only external factors — the only factors — that are not generated by the free choices of the market participants themselves are the laws of property and contract, which provide the structure within which economic choices are made and which do not necessarily correspond with what each individual would have chosen. If a political system could aggregate social preferences as well, social policy would be merely a matter of applying the appropriate aggregation device and ensuring that its results were followed.

Arrow's impossibility theorem tells us that such a utopian solution can never be attained. The difficulty is not that so far no one has had the ingenuity to devise the perfectly responsive political system. The difficulty is that, in a way that is not immediately self-evident, the concept of aggregating an unrestricted range of preferences without imposing some external constraints, either limiting the kinds of preferences or not giving equal weight to all participants' choices, involves an internal contradiction. Thus the aim of a social policy that is wholly determined only by the free choices of all citizens treated equally — so long as these choices do not happen to coincide or are not restricted by some procrustean rules — is a logical impossibility.

We can approach this problem of social choice from another angle. We can look at the problem as one of harmonizing the diversity of social values held by a heterogeneous society. Social values are reflected in what we choose to regard as natural rights or fundamental freedoms. The problem of reconciling these is very old — certainly as old as the American Constitution, whose framers were greatly concerned with reconciling what they regarded as natural rights with majority rule. Several years ago, in his *Preface to Democratic Theory,* Robert Dahl suggested that the problem of natural rights could be analyzed in terms of preferences of varying intensity. The distribution of preferences in any society can be plotted against both the proportion of the population holding a given belief and the intensity with which that belief is held. This seems to be a valuable way of analyzing the role of voluntary organization in a free society.

Simply counting the number of people with a given preference, which is all that a naive majoritarian system permits, runs the risk of overriding the intense preferences of a minority, that is, things that they regard as fundamental freedoms, with the weak preferences of the majority. Voluntary organizations to some extent enable a complex political system to adjust, in a way that the mere registering of a vote cannot, to this problem of the varying intensity with which preferences or value beliefs are held. By organizing themselves into a pressure group, the members of a minority who believe that some course of government action would infringe values or freedoms that they regard as fundamental can articulate those beliefs in a way that enables legislators and other agencies of government to take account of them and thus avoid the need for more desperate or violent forms of protest.

Nor is it only intense preferences or fundamental value beliefs that voluntary organizations can articulate. Where the members of a minority hold to some value that is not shared by their fellow citizens, they can act through voluntary organizations to advance those values themselves — so long, of course, as they do not conflict with the fundamental values of others. There are many examples of this: voluntary associations to support specific forms of education, of welfare services, of artistic endeavor, and so on. What is significant in both these cases is that, whereas government is the more efficient instrument where there is a measure of consensus, the role of Third Sector institutions is to add an element of diversity, enabling the society as a whole to respond to the greater range of values generated by a constellation of minorities.

Even so, the existence of a Third Sector cannot wholly resolve the problem of social choice that arises from a basic ambivalence in our concept of democratic freedom. Notably, it cannot enable the political system to resolve the impasse created where two sets of intense preferences or values held to be fundamental are in direct conflict. Moreover, the extent to which the Third Sector acts as a means of articulating the full range of values generated by a constellation of minorities is limited by two practical considerations. The most obvious is that all minorities are not equally able to establish voluntary associations so that the pluralist ideal is not, in practice, attained. Even if it were to be attained, the existence of voluntary associations is liable to make the reconciling role of government more difficult.

There is no satisfactory means of reconciling two conflicting sets of intense preferences. In practice, voluntary associations, and particularly single-issue lobbies, tend to intensify the preferences of their members and thus make an unresolvable preference distribution more likely. Voluntary associations do this both by stimulating their own members and by stimulating those with contrary beliefs to establish countervailing pressure groups of their own. Journalists have recently expressed concern about the spread of factionalism. This is characteristic of the political scene both in the United States and in Western Europe. This may in part be due to the increasing number of single-issue lobbies and groups. Nonetheless, I suspect that the increase of single-issue groups is more a symptom than a cause of factionalism. Factionalism seems to be due to a decline in the civic virtue of tolerance that cannot be fully explained merely by institutional changes.

What I have called the "categorical constraint" and what I continue loosely to call the "majoritarian constraint" seem to me to spring from essential characteristics of democratic government — the requirement of consent by the governed in the one case and the requirement of equal treatment in the other. Those who know government know that public administrators are also subject in practice to a number of other constraints that are not necessarily inherent in the very nature of democratic government. We know the tendency of government officials to think in terms of a relatively short time horizon, a constraint that springs from the fact that elections take place relatively frequently, and public officials are thus entrusted with responsibilities for relatively short periods at a time. We know their tendency to get caught in a morass of bureaucratic regulation that is often alienating to the very people it seeks to serve. These and some other constraints that offer Third Sector institutions scope to supplement and complement the activities of government are reviewed at the end of Chapter 8.

Finally, in the concluding chapter, I abandon the search for a truly comprehensive rationale for the Third Sector and illustrate instead some of the conclusions that may be drawn regarding the role and the accountability of the Third Sector from this partial rationale.

2

Defining the Bases of the Three Sectors

EXCHANGE AND AUTHORITY

Lindblom[1] maintains that "market systems are based on the exchange relation . . . government is similarly based on the authority relation." As he himself recognizes, this statement is not quite sufficient to define the base in either case. Exchange can be so broadly defined as to embrace all forms of social behavior (e.g., talking may be called an "exchange of words") that we must limit the form of exchange to what are usually called *quid pro quo* transactions.

The authority relation is even more difficult to define. Authority is to be found in almost every form of social organization, and we are looking for a form of authority that will help us distinguish the government sector from both the commercial and the nonprofit sectors. Neither "commands backed by prescribed penalties," which Dahl and Lindblom[2] adopted in an earlier work, nor Lindblom's present definition based on "pledged obedience"[3] will do for this particular purpose, since each of these forms of authority also exists in both the commercial and the voluntary nonprofit sectors.

Members of voluntary associations — for example, clubs, trade unions, professional associations — frequently accept the authority of specific officials (or committees) and recognize their right to prescribe penalties. Neither the rules nor the penalties in these cases can, however, normally be enforced by law otherwise than by contract.

Similarly, there are authority relations *within* firms of the commercial for-profit sector. It is quite a common problem for large firms in this sector to decide whether to produce components or raw materials themselves (vertical integration) or to buy them from outside suppliers. In the former case they rely on their *authority* over the constituent divisions of their enterprise to achieve the balance in the supplies they require. In the latter case they rely on the *quid pro quo* transactions of the market to supply the inputs for their own production. The relative merits of these two types of organization were influential in the development of the concept of transaction costs, which I discuss in the next chapter.

The authority exercised by a firm over its constituent divisions is not, any more than the authority exercised within voluntary associations, enforced by law, although indirectly it is ultimately enforceable by the law of contract. The *quid pro quo* transactions of the commercial sector are, of course, normally enforceable quite directly by the law of contract.

For our present purpose, therefore, I will identify the authority-relation characteristic of government with *commands liable to be enforced by law otherwise than as a matter of contract*. This definition of the distinctive nature of government authority emphasizes the role played by the law. I shall argue later that some of the limitations on the government sector arise from inherent characteristics of law.

What characterizes the Third Sector in the way that "exchange" characterizes the market sector and "authority" the government sector? I suggest that the key lies in "voluntary collective identification," and I shall try to explain what I mean by these three words.

INDIVIDUAL VERSUS COLLECTIVE RATIONALITY

In the market sector the relationship of participants is voluntary but self-seeking. Each actor freely enters into an exchange relationship but does so to advance his or her own interests. We say that a choice is "rational" in terms of market economics when in any transaction the *quid* received is equal to or greater than the *quo* foregone in terms of the individual's self-interest. In other words, to use a distinction drawn by Anatol Rapoport,[4] we may say that market economics is based on "*individual* rationality" as distinct from "*collective* rationality." The "invisible hand" argument tells us that, over a surprisingly wide range of circumstances, individual rationality pursued under conditions of perfect competition leads to collectively rational choices. Yet, as we shall see later when considering the cases of so-called market failure, there are various conditions in which the collectively rational choice cannot be reached by a series of individually rational market choices.

Society therefore needs a means of substituting collective rationality for individual rationality in cases in which individual rationality will not lead to collectively rational choices. This is the standard justification for government intervention when market outcomes can be shown to fall short of the collectively desirable outcome. Government achieves this objective by invoking the coercive authority of the law. The distinctive characteristic of voluntary organizations is that, either generally or for a limited purpose or for a limited group, they can pursue a collective good (even in some cases where it conflicts with their members' individual interests) without invoking the coercive authority of law.

In many forms of nonprofit organizations there is no conflict between the individual's self-interest and the collective interest of a wider group. Members of clubs, trade unions, professional associations, consumer and producer cooperatives, for example, rarely encounter a conflict between their own interests and that of the collectivity. They often see collective organization as the means of advancing their individual interests. Nonprofit organizations of this sort are probably best termed "mutual benefit organizations." They are often subject to legal provisions somewhat different than those that apply to "public benefit organizations" and in some ways resemble commercial sector organizations. Even in the case of mutual benefit organizations, however, what distinguishes these nonprofit organizations from market organizations is that they are structured in terms of the collective interest. Thus the member's identification with the collective interest is the basis of the relationship between the individual and the organization.

By identification with the collective interest, in this context, I merely mean the good on which the member can be assumed to focus. There is, of course, a sense in which for-profit organizations serve the public, but they also provide their members with a private benefit — a share in the profits — which nonprofit organizations cannot do. In the latter case it is *only* the collective good served by the organization on which the member can be assumed to focus. Even when the members share in the collective good, the good cannot be divided and shared among many. The collective good of the for-profit enterprise can be divided and distributed among the members, whereas the collective good of the nonprofit organization is indivisible even when the organization is established essentially to serve the selfish interests of its members. The members of an organization, such as a trade union established to raise wages for a particular craft or a trade body established to get tax advantages for a particular form of enterprise, obviously share in any collective good they manage to obtain, but they cannot divide that collective good up among themselves.

The fact that the good cannot be divided and nonmembers cannot be excluded from benefiting from it gives rise to the so-called *free rider problem* — the nonmembers who have made no sacrifices on behalf of the organization can take a "free ride" on the backs of the members who have borne the costs.

A special problem arises where the members do not themselves share in the good provided by the organization or where it can be shown that it is irrational in terms of the self-interest of the members of the organization to make the sacrifices entailed in membership. This is a problem to which I return later in discussing altruism.

The distinction between our three sectors of society on this analysis simply resolves itself into the product of two other distinctions:

(1) the distinction between an individual's pursuit of his or her own self-regarding good and his or her pursuit of the collective good of society (or a section of society) as a whole; and

(2) the distinction between voluntary pursuit of such a good and pursuit compelled by the coercive authority of law.

The market sector is based on the voluntary pursuit of self-interest; both the government sector and the voluntary sector are based on the pursuit of a collective good, but the former does so with coercive authority, the latter voluntarily. The coercive pursuit of self-interest presumably does not arise, since we have to assume that people do not require coercion in order to pursue their self-interest, at least so long as we assume that people are capable of identifying correctly their own interests.

SUMMARY

Following the Filer Commission, I have adopted the model of three sectors. I do not, however, wish to imply either that there are necessarily clear-cut distinctions between these sectors or that the constituents of one sector will always have more in common with each other than with the constituents of another sector. The decision as to whether to establish a small day care center as nonprofit or for profit may, for example, be almost arbitrary. A large nonprofit insurance undertaking, like the Teachers Insurance and Annuity Association (TIAA), may have more in common with commercial life insurance companies than with, say, a small welfare agency. The same problem arises in connection with the distinction between the nonprofit and for-profit sectors. A nationalized industry will normally be placed in the government sector and a privately owned (but publicly regulated) public utility company placed in the market sector. Yet the nationalized industry may have more in common with a privately owned public utility company — it may itself be a public utility — than with, let us say, a typical government service such as the Foreign Service. Similarly, the privately owned public utility, usually highly regulated, constrained in the ways it can pursue profits, and facing relatively weak competition, may have more in common with the nationalized public utility than with, say, a highly competitive firm in the garment trade. As John Simon often pointed out at seminars of the Yale Program on Non-Profit Organizations, we are really dealing with a "seamless web." At the boundaries between the three sectors the distinctions become blurred and almost arbitrary. In the final analysis, the boundaries are drawn by the form of incorporation — an artifact of the law — and in some cases the form of incorporation can be explained by little more than historical accident. Yet once we get away from the borderline cases, the distinctions are obvious enough.

When we speak of the constituents of any of the three sectors, we are really speaking of ideal types whose characteristics may obtain to a greater or lesser extent in any real institution. Economists usually take a small firm in a large competitive industry as the ideal type of constituent of the market sector. In much the same way, in what follows I shall take an institution that meets the legal requirements of charitable status in Anglo-American law as the ideal type in the nonprofit sector. These legal requirements are discussed in Chapter 4. Actual nonprofit organizations vary from this ideal type ranging from, at one extreme, those that are almost indistinguishable from commercial undertakings, such as certain mutual benefit clubs, to, at the other extreme, organizations that closely approximate government-provided public services, such as some of the larger welfare organizations.

3

Market Failure

The argument that is most often used both to justify government intervention and to explain the existence of a Third Sector that is neither dependent on the incentive profit nor subject to the disciplines of the market is based on the notion of so-called *market failure*. I find this argument suggestive but wanting, and I propose to offer some criticisms of it that seem to me fairly fundamental. However, before doing so, I need to review the argument itself if only for the benefit of those who are not already familiar with it.

THE PARETO OPTIMUM

Reconciling the aggregate of individual, self-regarding preferences with the collective good has been a central concern of economics at least since the time of Adam Smith. Analysis of the conditions under which the two coincide and under which when they do not (which has given rise to a considerable volume of highly technical literature in welfare economics) is probably most conveniently traced back to the work of Francis Edgeworth (1845-1926) and Vilfredo Pareto (1848-1923).

Edgeworth[1] introduced the distinction between *cardinal* utility — an absolute measure of a good — and *ordinal* utility — the relative place of a good in an individual's scale of preferences. Related to the distinction between cardinal and ordinal utility is the difficulty of making interpersonal comparisons of utility. We cannot get into each other's minds. If you and I are both having breakfast together and there is only one piece of toast left, can you or I really say which of us will get the greater satisfaction from the last piece of toast? What we can do is to say how each of us ranks our various wants and desires. We can do this in absolute terms — for example, a starving man in a warm climate is likely to rank food above clothing. But we can also get close to a relative measure by seeing how much of one thing an individual will prefer to how much of something else, and a good test of this is how much of the first thing the individual is prepared to exchange for how much of the second thing.

Pareto's[2] achievement was to find a way of making use of this fact to say something about the efficient distribution of resources in society without having to invoke any interpersonal comparisons of utility. Central to Pareto's conception of the efficient distribution of resources is the notion that an individual is made no worse off if he or she *voluntarily accepts* what he or she regards as adequate or more than adequate compensation for the loss of some benefit. If I voluntarily exchange one of my pieces of toast, which you want, for one of your spoonfuls of marmalade, which I want, we will both be better off and the distribution of resources at the breakfast table will be improved. When no further such exchanges of resources within the economy will improve the distribution of resources, we have reached a state of maximum efficiency, or, as it is now called, a Pareto optimum. There can be many such Pareto optima reflecting the range of combinations, each of which is optimal in the sense that it cannot be improved upon.

I think it is fairly clear that a Pareto optimum of this sort will define one conception of the "greatest good of the greatest number" and that this is the only definition that does not involve interpersonal comparisons of welfare. Needless to say, there are welfare economists who do not deny the possibility of interpersonal comparisons of welfare that, as scientific statements, interpersonal comparisons of welfare are unintelligible. There are some who take a "cardinalist" view of utility. There are also some who take an intermediate position between the pure "ordinalist" and the pure "cardinalist" view. Nonetheless, what I shall call "conventional economics" — and should more strictly be called "Paretian economics" — is based on the ordinalist view of utility.

Maurice Allais,[3] in his article on Pareto in the *International Encyclopedia of Social Sciences,* tells us that "Pareto went on to develop a line of argument, somewhat lacking in rigor, which showed that the state of maximum efficiency and a state of equilibrium under perfect competition are one and the same thing." In other words, markets operating under perfect competition will lead, if not absolutely, to the "greatest good of the greatest number," or at least to the nearest thing to that notion that makes sense if we deny the possibility of interpersonal comparisons of welfare. Subsequently, Pigou[4] and a whole constellation of economists have gone on not only to repair the "lack of rigor" in Pareto's argument but also, and is more relevant to our purpose, to define the conditions under which the equation of a market equilibrium with a Pareto optimum will not hold, which are now generally known as "market failures."

TYPES OF MARKET FAILURE

Pigou, in *Economics of Welfare,* provided the classic discussion of the conditions under which the free play of self-interest in the market may be expected to fail to maximize the collective good of the wider community. He gives a clear definition of one of the commonest forms of market failure: "One person A, in the course of rendering some service, for which payment is made, to a certain person B, incidentally also renders services or dis-services to other persons (not producers of like services), of such a sort that payment cannot be exacted from the benefitted parties or compensation on behalf of the injured parties."[5]

The term "market failure" may be somewhat confusing as we are used to thinking of "failures" in a very different context, as in the failure of a particular producer in the market for a particular class of goods. In this context, however, it refers to the failure of the market *system* to produce the most efficient outcome (in the Pareto sense) under certain conditions. It has nothing to do with failure in the bankruptcy sense and involves us in the rather difficult conceptual exercise of thinking about the characteristics of markets as a system for the allocation of resources. For a convenient, recent, and admirably succinct classification of what has become quite an extensive list of accepted market failures, I turn to a paper by Charles Wolf[6] called "A Theory of Non-Market Failure." He lists four categories of market failure:

- externalities and public goods
- increasing returns
- market imperfections
- distributional inequity

Externalities and Public Goods

Wolf defines externalities as "benefits or costs that are not, respectively, appropriable by, or collectible from, the producer." This is substantially the same as Pigou's definition. Externalities may be positive (e.g., environmental benefits that are not appropriable by the producer) or negative (e.g., environmental costs not collectible from the producer).

A group of developers who, by restoring houses in a rundown section of town, improve the whole area might be an example of people creating positive externalities. They can sell the houses they have restored and thus exact payment from the people to whom they sell those houses, but they may also have increased the value of other houses in the neighborhood (which they do not own), and they cannot collect from their owners any payment for the benefit they have brought to them. Conversely, a company setting up a messy or smelly works in the neighborhood might be an example of the creation of negative externalities. It has bought the site and thus paid for its use, but it cannot normally be made to compensate the neighbors for the damage it has done to their living conditions.

In practice, the neighbors would be likely to be protected (to some extent at least) by zoning laws and might even have some redress at common law. But neither of these would take the form of market transactions. This is what economists mean when they say that externalities and market failure "justify" intervention in the marketplace. Note, however, that the argument, in form, is an economic argument about efficiency, not a moral argument about justice. The problem for the economists is not that the works owners are being unfair to the neighbors, but that they are contributing to a less-than-optimal distribution of resources.

There are some goods and services whose benefits almost always take the form of positive externalities. These are the so-called pure public goods. An example of a pure public good would be a public park open to all. No charge is made for its use; the "producer," the benefactor who has established the park, has simply created a public good from which he or she derives no pecuniary benefit. The classic example of a public good is national defense. All citizens derive benefit from it, but it is impossible to devise any method by which the benefit can be paid for by the *quid pro quo* transactions of a market. As a result national defense has almost always been seen as a responsibility of the state, which can use taxation to coerce payment.

The problems raised by both public goods and positive externalities can be analyzed in terms of the "free rider" concept mentioned earlier. A free rider situation arises whenever the supplier of a good or service cannot capture sufficient benefits from his or her personal sacrifices although such sacrifices by many people simultaneously would yield large social benefits. In these circumstances some of the people who are benefiting are likely to prefer, rather than making sacrifices themselves, to take a free ride on the backs of those who are prepared to make sacrifices. The state discourages free riders by coercing payment through the tax system.

Where externalities are positive, too little output will be produced by market forces alone, and where externalities are negative, they will produce too much output — compared in both cases with Pareto-optimal output levels. For example, a steel works polluting the environment will find it economic to produce more steel if it does not have to pay for the damage it does to the environment (i.e., the cost remains *external* to the enterprise) than if it does have to pay the cost of the damage (i.e., when the costs are *internal* to the enterprise).

Increasing Returns

This is the classic case in which increasing returns and declining average costs will lead to monopolistic conditions:

A single producer can produce all or more than the market demands more cheaply than can several competing producers. The usual examples are the public utilities like gas, water, and electricity. Unless regulated such monopoly suppliers would be able to charge too much for the goods or services they provide.

Market Imperfections

Wolf uses this heading to describe all the other instances in which economic realities depart from the assumptions of a "perfect market" — where there are barriers to entry, where information is imperfect, where obstacles impede the mobility of resources, and so on.

Distributional Inequities

Wolf classes the tendency of the market system to result in a distribution of income or wealth that appears inequitable as a form of market failure. To me it seems a failing of a different kind. This is not so much a case of market forces proving incapable of attaining a Pareto optimum, but rather, I would argue that what we have here is an important failing of the Pareto concept itself, an idea to which I will return later.

Although, in the interests of lucidity, Wolf is surely right to have separate classes of market failure, all his examples (of cases where perfect market conditions will not necessarily attain a Pareto optimum) can be classed as externalities. For example, abuses of a monopoly position can be seen as a negative externality since a producer abusing his or her monopoly position will be externalizing costs that under competitive conditions would be internal, or internalizing benefits that would be external. Similar mental gymnastics can be used to bring into the category of externalities all the other forms. "Market failure," "public goods," "externalities," and, as we shall see in a moment, "transaction costs" are all flexible terms. They provide alternative forms of language in which we can express a whole range of rather similar ideas with which we are concerned when we consider the divergence between individual benefits and the collective benefit of a wider community.

THE LIMITED APPLICATION OF MARKET FAILURE BASED ON PARETO OPTIMALITY

It is convenient to limit the term "market failure" to those conditions in which it can be shown that free market conditions will be incapable of attaining a Pareto optimum. In so doing, we give the term a narrower technical meaning than that which "failure" bears in common parlance.

Not all the criticisms commonly made of the market system can be classed as market failures in this technical sense. Market failure would not include, for example, the cyclical tendency of the market system — that is, its tendency to swing between unemployment and inflation, let alone at times combining unemployment and price inflation.

Nor does market failure cover all the cases in which governments feel entitled to intervene in the operations of the market. Market failure, in this technical sense, will not provide a reason for subsidizing farmers, for preventing unemployment in declining industries, for nationalizing the "commanding heights of the economy," or for quite a few other instances of inroads that governments have, in fact, made into the economic marketplace.

What Pareto tried to show was that an economic system based on privately owned capital and perfect competition would have the same equilibrium state as one based on the aggregate economic preferences of the society *(maximum d'ophelimité pour la société)*.[7] The conventional lists of market failures, defined as demonstrable failures of the market to achieve Pareto optimality, are really no more than lists of the cases in which it can be shown that the argument used by Pareto (and his successors) involves a logical contradiction.

MARKET CONDITIONS: AN ARTIFACT OF THE LAW

The market failure argument is thus an a priori argument. Because market discipline is so often contrasted with government regulation, it is tempting to think of the conditions under which markets will operate properly as some sort of natural state to be contrasted with the artificiality of law. In fact, both market conditions and the conditions under which markets will not operate, that is market failures, are determined by the legal system.

All the cases of market failure listed above concern resources in which there are (or can be) no property rights (or, for some other reason, the laws of property and contract do not or cannot satisfactorily apply). Under market conditions, if A will be made better off by exchanging with B, something, say X, which he or she (A) wants for something B wants, say Y, both will be better off and the distribution of resources will obviously be better after the transaction than before it. X and Y can be either "goods" (including, of course, services, amenities, and so on) or "bads," but in any case there must be property rights in both X and Y.

The point is most obvious in the case of externalities, both positive and negative. Take first an example of a negative externality: If we imagine a situation in which the air we breathe is private property, in the same way as a house can be private property, there would be no need for clean air legislation to limit the negative externality of air pollution. Those who used and polluted air could be charged a market price by those who own it. However, in the real world, air cannot be sufficiently closely identified for me to be able to prove that the air I am breathing was polluted by the emissions from your car. So the cost to me of your car ruining "my" air is not something I can recover in any marketplace. On the other hand, if you want to use my house, ordinary market mechanisms are available: I can sell you the house; I can rent it to you; I can charge you for any damage you do to it; and so forth.

Similarly, take those examples of positive externalities that are "pure public goods," such as the benefits of national defense, an effective police force, a lighthouse to warn shipping, and so forth. In none of these cases can the provider of the service enforce a claim to property rights in the service he or she provides and charge for its use.

Armen Alchian puts the relationship of market mechanism to the concept of private property in its most extreme form.

> Every question of pricing is a question of property rights . . . the allocation of scarce resources in a society is the assignment of rights to uses of resources. So the question of economics, or of how prices should be determined, is the question of how property rights should be defined and exchanged and on what terms.[8]

The early classical economists themselves were well aware of the extent to which market conditions are an artifact of the law. Lionel Robbins, summarizing the attitude of the English classical political economists, wrote

> Thus so far from the system of economic freedom being something that will certainly come into being if things are

> just left to take their course, it can only come into being if they are not left to take their course, if a conscious effort is made to create the highly artificial environment which is necessary if it is to function properly. The "invisible hand" which guides men to promote ends which were no part of their intention is not the hand of some God or natural agency independent of human effort; it is the hand of the lawgiver.[9]

Kenneth Arrow also emphasizes the dependence of the market pricing system on the concept and the law of property. He adds the important rider that neither the market for private goods nor the pricing system can, by virtue of their dependence on the law, be sufficient if only because

> the course of the law itself cannot be regarded as subject to the price system. The judges and the police may indeed be paid, but the system itself would disappear if on each occasion they were to sell their services and their decisions.[10]

An incorruptible judiciary is not only a "public good"; it is a public good whose existence is presupposed by the market for private goods.

The difficulty of bringing a resource within the scope of the law of property may be a natural consequence of the nature of the goods as, for example, in the case of the service to shipping provided by a lighthouse. The information provided by the lighthouse is not something that can be made private property and for which a charge can be levied every time it is used. Or the difficulty may be an accidental, arbitrary consequence of the way the law of property in some particular state has developed. For example, in England, unlike, say, Italy or Connecticut, there are relatively few private beaches because English law makes it extremely difficult to enclose a private beach. Certainly there is no inevitable natural reason why beaches should normally be public, and the fact that access to beaches in England is usually a public right and not subject to a market price is simply the result of historical accident and of our legal traditions. Francis Bator[11] has emphasized the distinction between externalities that could, at least theoretically, be brought within the law of property (which he called Type I), such as English beaches, and those that could not, such as national defense.

If market conditions and hence market failures are an artifact of the law, can changes in the law remove market failure? To some extent they can. The reach of the law of property can change over time as technology and institutions change. Something that may at one period be a market failure may at another time be brought within the control of market forces by changes in the law or by technological developments. The boundaries of the market are not immutably drawn.

TRANSACTION COSTS

The fact that, by changes in the law of property (and by other institutional changes), we can shift goods and services between the public sector, the private market sector, and the Third Sector raises the question, how we can judge which sector is most appropriate — in which sector, subject to which discipline, will the service be most likely to be most efficiently carried out? This question is conveniently addressed by using the concept of "transaction costs." As with market failure, we are dealing with a technical term whose meaning may not be immediately apparent from the common usage of the words. The concept has been developed particularly by Oliver Williamson and Ronald Coase,[12] and in what follows I shall mostly follow Williamson's usage.

Williamson addresses a problem that often arises in large, for-profit organizations. Should the firm make a component itself or buy it from an autonomous supplier on the open market? In the former case — the component made by a wholly integrated division of the firm itself — the firm relies on its *authority* over the components division to get the components it requires to manufacture its final product. The quantity, the quality, the design, and other specifications of the components are all determined by *instructions* from the management of the firm. In the latter case, the firm relies on the operation of the market to obtain the components it requires.

These are two different kinds of transaction, each of which has a different set of advantages and disadvantages. The balance between the advantages and the disadvantages can be expressed as a cost, the cost of making use of one kind of transaction rather than the other. For example, in the case of a standardized part used by many other firms as well as by the firm itself, an autonomous supplier may be able to operate more cheaply by producing larger quantities of a given item for a bigger market than the one firm. This will also often be the case with raw materials. Conversely, particularly in the case of components that are highly specific to one firm, such as parts for a particular model of automobile, there may be many advantages in the firm's making the component itself. For example, the firm may thereby reduce transportation costs, achieve better control over volume and quality of component production, and so on. The firm can be expected to choose for each component the form of transaction in which transaction costs are the least, the form in which the balance between the advantages and disadvantages of the type of transaction is most favorable. In some cases, the lowest transaction costs may result from a mix of different types of transaction: for example, making some of the components itself with additional components bought out to meet unexpected peaks in demand.

Williamson does not confine his analysis to problems of manufacture. He notices that industries vary considerably in the extent to which they integrate their distribution networks. Some industries (such as packaged groceries and dry goods) leave both wholesaling and retailing to others. Other industries (such as tobacco) extend into wholesaling, while others (for example, sewing machines) do their own retailing. These involve different transaction costs: the relative advantages and disadvantages of relying on market transactions at different points in the distribution chain. Where retailing requires considerable point-of-sale information, such as with sewing machines, which may have to be demonstrated and serviced, the advantage lies, i.e., the transaction costs are least, in the firm maintaining its own specialized sales force. Where commodities are perishable and branded, firms move into wholesaling because of the difficulty of getting autonomous wholesalers to destroy stocks when these became old or spoiled in a way that would damage the manufacturer's reputation. When no such considerations apply, the advantage lie in using market transactions more extensively.

Transaction costs are not simply a matter of balancing prime costs. A manufacturer's decision about whether to buy or to manufacture a component itself does not depend simply on whether or not it can manufacture more cheaply than the outside contractor. All sorts of other considerations enter in: administrative costs, quality control, uncertainty in supply and demand, the risk of damage to goodwill, and so forth. Nonetheless, transaction costs viewed from the level of the firm remain relatively easy to express in dollar terms. When we move from the level of the firm to the level of society as a whole, the balance of advantages and disadvantages becomes more difficult to express in monetary terms.

Let us take television as an example of a service that is often provided under very different forms of transaction. Television can be provided as a public good by the state and paid for out of taxation. This is done in some countries. In

Britain, TV is partly provided by an independent, semi-autonomous public authority, the British Broadcasting Corporation, financed by a special tax, the license fee. Programs may also be produced as public goods by a nonprofit organization, like the American Public Broadcasting Service, raising money from donations and grants. Yet another alternative is the form of commercial broadcasting most common in the United States but also found in Britain and many other countries.

What the commercial American broadcasting companies sell is a private good — the right to include advertising messages with the broadcast program. So far as the viewing public is concerned, what they receive is a public good that fits Samuelson's definition that "each individual's consumption of that good leads to no subtraction from any other individual's consumption of that good."[13] The public good in this case is an externality — a benefit to viewers flowing from the market exchange transaction between the broadcasting company and the advertiser. The peculiar interest in this case is that the value of the private good is quite directly related to the externality it generates. This symbiosis between a private and a public good is not unique — there are several other examples in the field of advertising — but it is rare. It serves, however, to remind us that the distinction between private and public goods is an intellectual distinction and that the two may be quite difficult to distinguish in the real world. Finally, both cable and subscriber services using scrambling devices can provide a television service in a market situation almost entirely parallel to the competitive market for magazine subscriptions.

The relative advantages and disadvantages of operating a service either through the market, as in the case of cable TV; by voluntary effort, as in the case of American public service broadcasting; by a public authority, as a by-product of advertising; or in any of the other ways may be expressed as a hypothetical cost, a transaction cost analogous to the criteria used by a for-profit firm in deciding whether to buy components on the market or manufacture them itself. The trouble is that the transaction costs are considerably more difficult to express in dollar terms. Some transaction costs may be relatively easy to express in dollar terms. For example, the relative costs of cable and subscriber services using scrambling or metering devices are easily expressed in monetary terms. The relative transaction costs of cable versus advertising-based commercial TV can also probably be quantified relatively easily. We can assume that television provided by philanthropic endeavors, like PBS, will not, because of the free rider problem, reach Pareto optimal levels — although there is a major conceptual difficulty in the idea of a Pareto optimum for something like television. On the other hand, can we put a dollar figure on the political dangers of television provided as a public service by the government?

Historically, an important example of a collective good transformed into a private good by changes in the law of property is provided by the enclosures of the commons in eighteenth-century England. The common lands in question were originally public goods. All villagers were entitled to graze their flocks on the commons. This did not necessarily lead to optimal use. Each villager would rationally increase the livestock he or she kept on the commons. However, beyond a certain point, because of overgrazing, the total amount of stock the commons could support would be reduced. The more each villager pursued his or her own interests, the poorer the village as a whole would become. This has been used as a prototype of many similar conservation problems and is sometimes called the "commons dilemma," a variant of the "prisoner's dilemma," beloved of game theorists, where the collective interest of the group conflicts with the individual interests of the groups' members. It is quite easily analyzed in terms of externalities.

The problem, the conflict between individual and collective interests, arises because of a negative externality — the damage done by overgrazing was external and not collectible from the villagers who put their flocks out to graze. The problem disappeared when the commons began to be enclosed by act of Parliament, that is, turned into private property. This process was, however, far from cost free. Indeed, the cost of the enclosures, in terms of human misery and the disruption of village life, was so great we can hardly imagine it being repeated today. The application of the concept of transactions costs is also fairly clear: The transaction cost of keeping the commons as a collective good was the cost of overgrazing; the cost of making grazing rights into a market transaction was the misery caused by the enclosures. The real historical cases are, of course, complicated by a vast number of other factors — the adequacy of compensation for the loss of villagers' rights, the availability of alternative forms of employment, and so on — but this illustration may serve to show how the concept of transaction costs can be used. As with the television example, the difficulty in using the concept lies less in the application of a very flexible concept but than in the difficulty of finding units (whether dollars or otherwise) that can be used to measure very different kinds of costs that in the worst case may represent incommensurables.

A very wide range of goods and services could, in pure theory, be allocated to any of the three sectors. Admittedly it may tax the imagination to think of extreme cases of public goods, like national defense, being adequately supplied by voluntary action or of any means of bringing its benefits into marketable form. But many other forms of public goods — highways, police services, street lighting, fire services, drainage, parks, libraries, and so on — could be, have been, and, in some cases, still are found in any of the three sectors. Similarly, it is possible to think of ways of bringing many of the problems of pollution and conservation within the control of market forces by extending the reach of private property. Conversely, we can think easily enough of many private goods (e.g., water supply and utilities) that could conceivably be turned into public goods and provided by government out of the fund of taxation. The British National Health Service is a fairly recent example of such a transfer from one sector to another. In some cases the allocation to one sector rather than another seems no more than a historical accident.

Transaction Costs versus Externalities

It hardly needs saying that all forms of market failure can be expressed and analyzed in the language of transaction costs, which, indeed, has a number of advantages. Unlike the dichotomous pair of "public" versus "private" goods, it emphasizes the graduated nature of the choice between supply through a commercial market, through voluntary action, through coercive government action, or through combinations and intermediate forms of these methods. Transaction costs language provides a conceptual tool for analyzing such choices. It points more precisely than the language of externalities to the particular weakness in the market that causes its failure. Perhaps above all, it emphasizes the importance of the definition of the participants to a transaction. Externalities arise when not all those affected by a transaction have participated in it. In the terms of Pigou's definition quoted above, the transaction between A and B is providing services or disservices to others who are not parties to the transaction: They are benefited or injured parties, but they are not parties to the transaction. It is more or less difficult—which an economist translates as "more or less costly"—for them to be permitted to enter the transaction. Nonetheless, at this stage, I propose to remain with the language of externalities. My present concern is to set forth the failure characteristics of institutions of the three sectors in black and white terms. It is when we reach the gray area of goods and services that shift between institutions of the three sectors that we need the language of transaction costs.

It should perhaps also be pointed out that not all problems of resource allocations can be satisfactorily solved by any of our three methods of resource allocations — government, market, and voluntary action — or by any of our three sectors either in isolation or combination. Calabresi and Bobitt,[14] in a sensitive and humane study, have pointed to a class of tragic dilemmas in which none of the methods of allocation will seem satisfactory. Such dilemmas arise, for example, when the allocation of a scarce resource — such as a kidney or organ transplant — directly determines who will live and who will die. They argue that the different methods of allocation embody different values and that such "tragic choices" will arise whenever society is faced by conflicting fundamental values. Another way of expressing this is to say that they are choices between incommensurables. In the last analysis, there is really no way in which we can relate the value of one life to another.

THE MARKET FAILURE RATIONALE FOR NONMARKET OPERATIONS

Such, in summary form, are the market failure arguments. How do they bear on the principal concern of this book, the need for a Third Sector? Charles Wolf tells us that "it is almost a truism that the principal rationale for public policy intervention lies in the inadequacies of market outcomes." He could have added that such market failures are almost as often offered as the rationale for the intervention of the voluntary nonprofit sector. Burton Weisbrod[15] and Susan Rose-Ackerman[16] treat public sector and voluntary nonprofit sector production as two alternative responses to the problem of supplying public goods. Roland McKean sees the voluntary nonprofit organization as an exercise by which the member fights the temptation to become a "free rider."[17] Nelson and Krashinsky[18] and Henry Hansmann[19] offer a rationale for a Third Sector based on another form of market failure — one of Wolf's miscellaneous categories of market imperfections — where consumers, lacking sufficient information to control the quality of the product, fear that they will be exploited by a for-profit organization and therefore seek the added safeguard of the nonprofit form. All these market failures can be expressed in terms of externalities. For convenience, I will deal first with the general form of the argument under the heading of "public benefit" and, subsequently, with a particular form of externality under the heading of "failure to trust in the market."

The concern of this book is not, of course, with the rationale for government policy but with the rationale for private nonprofit organizations and, in particular, for those nonprofit organizations that can be classified as "charitable." However, the arguments from market failure apply equally to the rationale for government intervention and for charitable action. I can therefore distinguish the rationale for private charity from the rationale for government intervention only after discussing the arguments that apply to both. In the next chapter I start by reviewing the legal definition of charity, but I find that the economic justification for that definition is virtually identical to the economic justification for government intervention. In consequence, the next three chapters will be primarily concerned with arguments that apply to both government and nonprofits, and it is only from Chapter 7 onward that I try to distinguish the case for private nonprofits from the case for government intervention.

4

The Public Benefit Argument

I am taking a charitable institution as the ideal type of Third Sector institution, believing that the characteristics of charities will be the most easy to distinguish from the characteristics of both commercial undertakings and government agencies. Yet even so, the question "what is a charity?" is quite surprisingly difficult to answer.

HISTORICAL DEFINITIONS: ENGLISH AND AMERICAN LAWS OF CHARITY

In common parlance, we use the term to denote an institution that is somehow involved in "good works" — usually helping the poor or otherwise disadvantaged — but we find it difficult to be much more precise. The lawyers have developed their own use of the term, which in some ways is quite significantly different from the way the term is used in everyday speech. Quite a few institutions that are charities by law would not be immediately recognized as charities by the individual in the street, and occasionally we find institutions that are refused charitable status which the layperson would think of as charitable. Although the lawyers have been wrestling with the problem for centuries, they have not been able to define precisely what are the both necessary and sufficient conditions for charitable status. This is because charitable status is to some extent an open-ended concept that changes over time as social circumstances change. In early times lawyers of the Anglo-American common law tradition needed to identify charities because only charitable trusts could be established in perpetuity. Today legal definitions are needed to identify charities more often because charities enjoy considerable tax advantages.

Although the lawyers may not have devised and probably will never be able to find a fully comprehensive definition, they have managed to identify some of the essential characteristics of charity. One of these characteristics is the fairly obvious one that a charity is not established merely for the benefit of its own members, that it is not, as they say, self-dealing.

The other essential characteristic, closely related to this, in both the English and American law of charities, is that a charity produces a significant amount of benefit to the community as a whole or to a significant part of the community. *The Restatements of the Law of Trusts*[1] states for American law that "a purpose is charitable if its accomplishment is of such social interest to the community as to justify permitting property to be devoted to the purpose in perpetuity." Similarly *Halsbury's Laws of England*[2] states that "in determining what purposes are charitable, the Court has always applied the over-riding test of public benefit." Clearly this legal concept of public benefit is akin to the economic concept of transactions generating positive externalities.

For the purpose of administering the charitable exemption from federal income tax, the Internal Revenue Service authorities have had to go beyond these very general statements and describe what nonprofit organizations would be recognized as "of such social interest to the community" as to fall within the concept of charity. Section 501 (C)(3) of the

Internal Revenue Code tells us that such organizations must be "organized exclusively for religious, charitable, scientific, testing for public safety, literary or educational purposes, or for the prevention of cruelty to children or animals." With the possible exception of "testing for public safety," all these purposes would come within the broader legal definition of charity. With some duplication the term "charitable" is further elucidated in the Regulations, which state that the term "charitable" includes

> relief of the poor and distressed or of the underprivileged; advancement of religion; advancement of education or science; erection or maintenance of public buildings, monuments, or works; lessening of the burdens of government; and promotion of social welfare by organizations designed to accomplish any of the above purposes, or (1) to lessen neighborhood tensions; (2) to eliminate prejudice or discrimination; (3) to defend human and civil rights secured by law; or (4) to combat community deterioration and juvenile delinquency.[3]

U.S. tax regulations do not pretend to provide a comprehensive, all-inclusive catalogue of purposes that would be recognized as charitable. They merely give a list of purposes that would be included in the "generally accepted legal sense" of charity.

The list can trace a respectably ancient lineage going back at least to the famous "index or chart" of instances of charitable purposes given in the Preamble to the Elizabethan Statute of Charitable Uses of 1601.[4] The English courts still use the "spirit and intendment" of this Elizabethan preamble in determining charitable status despite attempts[5] to get the legislature to provide more up-to-date illustrations of charitable purposes. The purposes set out in this preamble are, in modernized English, as follows:

> the relief of aged, impotent and poor people; the maintenance of sick and maimed soldiers and mariners, schools of

> learning, free schools and scholars in universities; the repair of bridges, ports, havens, causeways, churches, sea-banks and highways; the education and preferment of orphans; the relief, stock or maintenance of houses of correction; the marriages of poor maids, the supportation, aid and help of young tradesmen, handicraftsmen and persons decayed; the relief or redemption of prisoners or captives; and the aid or ease of any poor inhabitants concerning payment of fifteens, setting out of soldiers and other taxes [43 Eliz. I. c. 4].

The Elizabethan preamble is in no way a definition of charity. It is essentially a catalogue of some purposes that were at the time recognized as charitable, and the courts have proceeded by drawing analogies with those purposes and, in recent times, quite often by analogies with the analogies. The list in the Elizabethan preamble has been so influential in determining the development of the concept of charity in both English and American law that it is worth looking at closely to see how far the purposes listed therein and some more recent examples that are held to be analogous would be covered by the economic concepts of market failure and externalities. Let us see into what economic categories we can classify the illustrations listed in the Elizabethan preamble (without following the order in which they appear in the preamble).

MARKET FAILURE AND EXTERNALITIES

Pure Public Goods

First, we find several examples of what economists would recognize as "pure public goods." These are goods that have to be made available without charge. It is impossible to exclude anyone from their use, and they usually are of such a nature that one person's use of them does not detract from anyone else's use of them.

Certainly under the conditions of the time, it would have been impossible to exclude, and hence levy a charge on, those using bridges, ports, havens, causeways, seabanks, and highways. Churches may be very nearly in the same category. These examples are interesting because it is striking how many of them have subsequently moved out of the charitable sector. Some, for a time — for example, commercial toll roads and bridges — moved into the market sector, but most by now have ended up in the government sector. This historical tendency suggests that Susan Rose-Ackerman[6] is right in suggesting that, because of the free rider problem, provision of such public goods by voluntary nonprofits is likely to be less efficient than is supply by the public sector, which can coerce payment of the cost.

Nonetheless, quite a few contemporary functions of philanthropy still fit the category of pure public good. I have already mentioned the case of public service broadcasting — both radio and television. Similarly, the fruits of scientific research are goods such that each individual's use of that knowledge leads to no subtraction from any other individual's use of it. (This holds so long as people are not excluded from their use, for example, by patients.) Some of the newer categories listed in the Treasury Department regulations — such as lessening neighborhood tensions or combating community deterioration and juvenile delinquency — may also be classified as pure public goods in that it is impossible to exclude people from their benefits.

Positive Externalities

Second, we find examples of goods and services which, while they do not satisfy the criterion of nonexcludability, nonetheless fit the broader category of goods generating significant externalities. Educational resources are limited. Each individual's use of them does reduce the resources available for other individuals. People can be and are excluded — on many grounds — from the use of educational resources, especially in poor countries. The same is true of art and literature, except for the relatively unusual forms of art that are available free to all. To include these, we have to extend our definition to include positive externalities, in other words, beneficial spillover effects on the rest of society. We can do this well within the market failure rationale based on Pareto optimality. If we assume that education benefits not only the people receiving the education but society as a whole, we can show that education, subject only to the market discipline of recovering the full value of the benefit conferred from those who receive the education, will be provided to less than the Pareto optimum. This enables us to include another whole range of functions undertaken both currently and in the past by philanthropic institutions. Health would be a major area of philanthropic activity that can be seen partly as a case of pure public goods and partly as an activity carrying positive externalities. Public health, such as sanitary measures designed to stop the spread of communicable diseases, are clearly pure public goods; but even where the delivery of medical services is to specific beneficiaries, there may be a sense in which health, like education, may be seen as a benefit spilling over beyond the immediate beneficiaries into society as a whole.

Eleemosynary Charities

However, having allowed for these two categories that clearly fit the concepts of public goods and positive externalities, we still find a crucially important third set of charitable purposes that I find difficult to fit into any category of economic externalities or, indeed, into any theory of market failure based on Pareto optimality. These are the eleemosynary purposes illustrated by the "relief of aged, impotent and poor people" and, in modern times, any number of welfare organizations designed for the relief of poverty. Interestingly enough, they also present a problem for the lawyers. Hubert Picarda, for example, states that "in the case of gifts for the relief of poverty, the requirement of public benefit is not essential or is at least modified."[7] The problem that worries Picarda (and which often seems to have been glossed over by other writers) is that the poor is a limited class of the public and is frequently further limited by the gift, e.g., to the poor of a particular parish or the victims of a particular disaster. The benefit to the recipient of the alms is self-evident; the benefit to the community as a whole is not.

My own difficulty is somewhat different. I have defined both market failure and externalities in relation to Pareto's criterion of efficiency, which is based on exchange and self-regarding preferences. Pareto not only assumes perfect competition (which is probably rare in practice); his theorems also depend on the assumption that the initial distribution of property and wealth necessarily maximizes collective welfare. This, of course, is by no means necessarily true. Moreover, if the initial distribution of property is unfair or fails to maximize collective welfare, the transactions on which Pareto relies to reach his state of maximum efficiency may actually exaggerate the initial inequities.

Wolf[8] makes an ingenious attempt to treat the tendency of free market forces to result in an apparently inequitable distribution of wealth and income as a form of market failure. His argument is that an equitable distribution of income is a particular type of public good. The voluntary sector possesses only one source of supply of that good — philanthropy or charity. However, since philanthropy and charity yield benefits that are not appropriable by the donors, the "production" of philanthropic redistribution will fail — like the production of any other public good or commodity carrying positive externalities — to attain its Pareto optimum level as a result of market forces alone. This seems to me an overingenious argument. The Pareto optimum is based on the concept of exchanges in which each participant is adequately compensated for the sacrifices he or she makes, but redistribution by its very nature implies a transfer of resources that must *not* be adequately compensated (at least in material terms). The producers of other forms of public goods cannot be adequately compensated, but if it were possible, it would not be illogical.

Compare Wolf's idea of "distributional equity" as a public good with a more usual public good, say, clean air. A desire for clean air can be an ordinary, self-regarding preference. It so happens that in the real world it is technically impossible to price the value of clean air, but if it were possible, we could see where it would fit into the ordering of consumer preferences, and this would be the Pareto optimum — even though it is unquantifiable in the real world. The relief of poverty, on the other hand, is not a self-regarding preference. There is nothing technically impossible in consumers expressing in terms of voluntary transaction where, in their ordering of preferences, they place the relief of poverty. The difficulty is that so long as we confine ourselves to ordinal utility, that is to say, abjure any possibility of making interpersonal comparisons of utility, and rely on the willingness of people to exchange the goods they own in order to achieve the optimum distribution of resources, we can have no criterion of the optimum distribution of property and wealth. We have gone beyond the limits of economics and entered the realm of moral philosophy. We must rely on some theory of distributive justice and not on the aggregation of individual, self-regarding preferences.

Wolf's attempt to bring distributional equity into conventional economic analysis is clearly well intended but fails because the Paretian analysis is too restricted.

ALTRUISM AS A SELF-REGARDING PREFERENCE

It is quite true that altruism and philanthropy may have self-regarding elements. These are of several kinds. Robert H. Bremner, for example, suggests that there may have been an element of self-interest — or to be more accurate, the group self-interest of millionaires — in Andrew Carnegie's philanthropies. He suggests that in part Carnegie saw philanthropy "as an antidote for radical proposals for redistributing property and a method of reconciling the poor and the rich."[9] The individual may derive satisfaction him- or herself from helping others — in the jargon of economics, that satisfaction enters into the utility function of the giver. Guido Calabresi subtly distinguishes at least four varieties of altruism that in different ways may be viewed as "a commodity which has value in our individual preference functions."[10] These vary from the pleasure one individual may get from another's well-being to the generalized pleasure any individual may get from the knowledge that he or she lives in a society of mutual charity and trust.

If we could include desires about the sort of society in which we wish to live among the "commodities which have value in our individual preference functions," we could extend the market failure rationale to include a host of functions undertaken by public and private philanthropy. The healthy may wish to live in a society that cares for the sick; the rich may wish to live in a society that succors the poor; the well-housed may wish to live in a society that houses the homeless; and so on. In this way, social and welfare services become public goods carrying positive externalities in the same way as do national defense, highways, education, and the like. Because the providers of these services cannot fully appropriate the benefits, market forces alone will produce less than optimal levels of such services. Note that this argument depends not on the benefits derived by the immediate beneficiaries — the sick, the poor, the homeless, and so forth — but on the indirect and irrecoverable benefits to those who place a value on that type of society. If we were only concerned with the direct beneficiaries, the Pareto optima would be reached by market forces, assuming, of course, that there was perfect competition in the supply of these services and, *per impossible,* that the initial distribution of property was perfectly equitable.

Note also that these "altruistic beneficiaries" may be in the "free rider" position. Without themselves contributing to the relief of the poor, those who want to live in a society that succors the poor may take a free ride on the back of those philanthropists who contribute to the relief of poverty. It is because she fears that many will do just this that Susan Rose-Ackerman maintains that social services financed by voluntary contributions will be less efficient — in the Pareto sense — than publicly financed services.

But are we entitled to extend the economists' concept of the individual utility or preference function to include altruistic desires, in this way? Amartya K. Sen[11] draws a distinction that seems to me to answer this question. He distinguishes forms of altruistic behavior that enter into one's own utility function — "pleasure at another's pleasure and pain at another's pain" — from altruistic choices that do not contribute to one's personal welfare and may actually run counter to it. The former he calls "sympathy" and the latter "commitment." Sympathy can be explained by suitably extending the conventional economic analysis based on the assumption that each individual will seek to maximize his or her personal welfare; commitment cannot, but requires the introduction of a different moral criterion for choice. Sen's concept of commitment comes very close to the doctrine preached by many Christian moralists that charity or love requires sacrifice. Merely giving to others goods we do not want, or from our superabundance, may satisfy the lawyers' concept of charity but not the moralists'. "You must give until it hurts" is a favorite theme of Lenten sermons.

Sen's desire to limit conventional economic analysis to self-regarding preferences, leaving the study of truly altruistic behavior to other disciplines (or to some sort of meta-economics), seems to me sound. Economics has gone far by assuming that in most cases actors within the economy will seek the rational way to advance their selfish interests. Adam Smith's central insight — that if each of us is free to pursue his or her own selfish interests in untrammeled competition we will also be serving best the public weal — must be one of the most striking-seeming paradoxes in the history of thought and was, certainly one of the most influential. Greed is a powerful instinct, and a discipline based on the assumption that it will be rationally pursued will go far to explain human behavior.

Yet it is not the only instinct with which humans are endowed. Any of us seeing a child drowning will rush to try and rescue him or her, certainly at the cost of getting our clothes wet and quite probably, in many cases, at the risk of our own lives. We may be under no legal obligation to do so. We are not seeking our own welfare. On the contrary, we almost certainly incur some slight economic cost and possibly a very large one.[12] One can argue that the fact that we chose to try to save the child's life proves that we prefer the moral gratification it gives us to the cost of sending our clothes to the dry cleaners. The concept of a preference function *can* be extended to cover any observed preference, whether self-seeking or altruistic, but only at the cost of tautology. Economic actors will choose according to their preference function, and their preference function is defined as what they choose. It is to avoid such a circular definition of "economic preference" that Sen introduces his distinction.

The point that is of more immediate relevance to our present purpose is that such a circular definition of economic preference would destroy the concept of market failure. Market failures are not observed malfunctions like engine failure. Indeed, since neither the Pareto optimum nor the value of most externalities can be measured, market failure is incapable of being an observed phenomenon. The concepts of market failure and of externalities are logical deductions from the assumption of self-regarding preferences. It is because we assume that producers act in accordance with their self-regarding preferences that we can conclude that where producers cannot appropriate all the benefits, production will fall short of the Pareto optimum.

Economists will, I think, always have difficulty with eleemosynary charity. The concepts of exchange and the self-regarding preference are deeply ingrained in economics and both are virtually excluded by the definition of alms — "gifts made without the expectation of reciprocity." The lawyers, of course, have recognized the place of alms in charity from the very beginning, but they do not need to explain either the motivation or the social purpose.

The relief of poverty is not the only charitable purpose recognized by the law. As early as 1891, Lord MacNaghten, in a judgment that classified charitable purposes and deeply influenced the development of both English and American law on charities, pointed out that a charity may be no less charitable because it benefits the rich as well as the poor "as indeed every charity that deserves the name must do either directly or indirectly."[13] Similarly, the fact that an organization makes a charge for its service does not necessarily preclude it from being a charity. A university or a school does not lose its charitable status when it charges fees, nor does a museum or an art gallery when it charges admission. What charities have to show is that, as well as being nonprofit, they are organized for a purpose that is of public benefit. The legal concept of public benefit is remarkably similar to — although narrower than — the economic concept of a positive externality. The benefits must not be fully captured by the *quid pro quo* but must spill over into society at large. The law does not demand the total absence of any *quid*.

MUTUAL PRIVATE BENEFIT

There are, however, many nonprofit organizations that are not charities. The nonprofit form is often used by organizations established for the private benefit of the members, not for any public benefit. Social clubs are frequently established as nonprofit organizations even when they have no charitable objectives. They are organized for the benefit of their members. The contributors and the beneficiaries are essentially the same people. The same is true of trade unions, mutual funds, and any number of professional and business groups established as nonprofit organizations for the benefit of their members. In many cases (but not all) the nonprofit form is adopted because of the difficulty of charging for the organization's services, such as the impossibility of excluding people from the benefits. This would be true of a trade union, which can hardly prevent nonmembers from benefiting from any concessions it has negotiated. It would not be true, on the other hand, of most social clubs, which theoretically could easily charge for entrance to the premises.[14] None of these organizations that lack the element of public (as opposed to private) benefit qualify as charities —

although some of them may enjoy tax privileges under other headings than the law of charities. The idea of charity implies, at least to some extent, the idea of helping others. It seems common sense, therefore, that the donors and the beneficiaries should not be the same people.

Yet even this principle — that the beneficiaries should be different from the donors — presents a problem in one class of cases. It is now generally recognized that the best way of helping people suffering from some physical or social disability is by organizations consisting of people suffering themselves from the same disability. Alcoholics Anonymous and many similar self-help organizations would be examples. Clearly, if the organization provides its services to all suffering from the disability, whether or not they are members, the organization (always assuming it meets the other requirements) would be entitled to charitable status. But if the organization provides its services only to members, should it lose its claim to charitable status, even though the individual in the street might consider the members to be charitable cases? In England, an organization called *Gingerbread* was set up to establish such a network of self-help groups for single-parent families. It was refused charitable status by the Charity Commission.

POLITICAL VERSUS CHARITABLE BENEFITS

These cases of "deserving" self-help organizations — which the layperson might think ought to be charities but which are not recognized as charities by the law — are probably quite few. The class of nonprofit organizations established for the private benefit of their members (not the public benefit) — and which both layperson and lawyer alike would regard as not entitled to charitable status — is very large. There is one important class of nonprofit organizations, moreover, that *are* established for public benefit but that are *not* charities. These are political organizations. They range from the political parties themselves through a whole variety of lobbies and interest groups.

English and American law on the point is essentially the same in principle.[15] The English principle can be stated quite simply: A trust for the attainment of political objectives is not charitable.[16] The American tax law and regulations spell out the principle in greater detail: Nonprofit organizations that are not entitled to tax exemption as charities by virtue of their political objectives or activities are called "action organizations" by the Internal Revenue Service. "Engaging in any of the three following activities can lead to classification as an action organization: (1) attempting to influence legislation, (2) participating in a political campaign and (3) having a primary objective that may only be attained by legislation or defeat of proposed legislation."[17]

In a sense, the attempt to distinguish political from charitable objectives borders on paradox. In the broadest sense of the word, anything connected with the public interest or the public benefit is "political." Moreover, as we have already seen, the charitable sector often runs parallel to the public sector. All told, it is not surprising that the borderline between charitable and political objectives should be a controversial frontier.

Where a charitable organization provides a public benefit that the state does not provide, or where the benefit provided by a charitable organization lessens the burdens on the public purse, few people would question its entitlement to charitable status. This would be the case with most charities established before this century. The philanthropists in the nineteenth century and earlier seem to have seen their role essentially as using their own resources to alleviate some distress that they wished to alleviate or provide some other social benefit that they felt to be needed. In this century, with the expanded role of the state and particularly the development of statutory welfare services, voluntary organizations have often seen their role in wider terms. The English Charity Commissioners have described how this development came about.

> Many organizations now feel that it is not sufficient simply to alleviate distress arising from particular social conditions or even to go further and collect and disseminate information about the problems they encounter. They feel compelled also to draw attention as forcibly as possible to the needs which they think are not being met, to rouse the conscience of the public to demand action and to press for effective official provision to be made to meet those needs.[18]

The attitude of such voluntary organizations is very understandable. Their resources are limited. In many cases their resources are manifestly inadequate to deal with the magnitude of the problems they encounter. Would it not be far more effective, rather than using their resources to tinker with the edges of the problem, to use those resources to stimulate a substantial government program capable of making a significant impact on the problem? But if they do so, have they not become political organizations?

The argument that when a charity's activities lessen the burden on government they should enjoy tax privileges is easy to understand. However, when the organization's activities are directed not at lessening but at increasing the burden on the taxpayer, is it fair that the organization should be able to use tax-exempt funds for this purpose? Some have argued that it is not. Others maintain that so long as the objective is manifestly charitable — the relief of poverty, the advancement of education, the elimination of prejudice and discrimination, and so on — it should be legitimate for voluntary organizations to use tax-exempt funds to advocate changes in public policy even when these changes would increase the burden on others.[19] They point out incidentally that the organizations opposing such changes in public policy are often themselves able to use funds that have not been taxed (for example, contributions that are allowable as business expenses). Moreover, in practice, it can be difficult to decide whether an organization's primary objective involves legislation or whether this is only a secondary objective, whether giving evidence to a congressional committee constitutes an "attempt to influence legislation" and similar borderline problems. Frankly, neither English nor American law has been particularly successful in drawing an entirely clear frontier between charitable and political activity.

The whole question of the distinction between political and charitable objectives is closely connected to the pluralistic or polyarchal theory of democracy that I discuss in Chapter 8. Nonetheless, there is an important theoretical distinction between the role of charities in a pluralist democracy adding to the range of values expressed by the political system and the role of nonprofit organizations that seek to alter or amend the values the political system expresses. Although in borderline cases it may be quite difficult to say on which side of this divide a particular organization falls, in general the role of charities is recognized as the former, not the latter. Certainly, an organization whose primary purpose was to support candidates for political office or to change the law would not be a charity but rather either a political party or an "action organization." Both could be and generally are nonprofits.

5

The Concept of Self-Interest

The concept of self-interest permeates the social sciences. Albert Hirschman has traced, in *The Passions and the Interests,* the way in which the idea of society held together by the self-love of its members — rather than the earlier normative concept of society held together by charity or fellow-love — gradually, over the seventeenth and eighteenth centuries, came to occupy the central place, first, in political theory and, subsequently, in the newly emerging discipline of economics. Economists from the time of Adam Smith onward have assumed that each participant in the economy is motivated by the thought of his or her own gain. Similarly, political theorists and sociologists generally look for self-regarding motives for social actions.

Yet the concept of self-interest raises the question of what is the self in relation to which the individual judges the gain. The pure egoist who would judge his or her interest exclusively in relation to a solipsist concept of him- or herself is probably quite rare. Most people's concept of their own interest extends to embrace at least the nuclear family. The tax accountant recognizes this when, for example, he or she aggregates the income of husband and wife or refuses to allow the income of dependent children to be assessed separately to progressive taxation. Lawyers will occasionally use the term "self-dealing" for transactions that illegally or unfairly benefit close relatives. Statisticians speak of household budgets and often average wealth or income over the number of households rather than literally per capita. Politicians and trade union negotiators speak of the level of wages required to maintain a family. In practice, it is relatively rare to find the solipsist self used as the economic unit.

SYMPATHY AND SELF-INTEREST

Adam Smith himself was well aware of the extent to which humans not only do but, above all, *should* act in ways that are not purely self-regarding. In *The Theory of Moral Sentiments,* he based his whole theory of morals on the concept of sympathy. Adam Smith's concept of sympathy, unlike Sen's, is not differentiated from commitment but rather includes both "sympathy" and "commitment" in Sen's meaning of those terms. Our senses reveal only a solipsist self and can give us no immediate experience of what other people feel. "Though our brother is upon the rack, as long as we ourselves are at our ease, our senses will never inform us of what he suffers." Our senses leave us, as it were, in a solipsist prison. But we can break out of that prison by imagination. "By imagination we place ourselves in his situation; we conceive ourselves enduring all the same torments." Nor is sympathy engendered merely by circumstances creating pain or sorrow: "Whatever is the passion which arises from any object in the person principally concerned, an analogous emotion springs up at the thought of his situation, in the breast of every attentive spectator."[1] It is clear that Adam Smith, who had written *The Theory of Moral Sentiments* before he wrote *The Wealth of Nations,* knew quite well that self-interest would not explain all human behavior.[2]

Economic behavior could be explained by narrow self-interest alone; moral behavior could not. To explain what he called our "benevolent affections," which he regarded as constituting "the perfection of human nature," we had to refer ourselves to something wider than the self of which our senses made us aware. This we could do through imagination and sympathy. Two centuries later, we probably cannot greatly improve on imagination and sympathy as the motivating force behind charity that enables us to identify with others, to feel in some measure what they feel, to suffer at their hurt, to resent those who betray them, to rejoice at their joy.

The distinction between self-interested economic behavior and altruistic behavior based on charity does not, however, correspond to the distinction between the for-profit commercial sector and the nonprofit sector. Self-interested behavior even in the economic sense can exist within the nonprofit sector.

SEPARATE AND SELECTIVE INCENTIVE

Mancur Olson has provided in *The Logic of Collective Action* an explanation of how nonprofit groups might be formed to pursue collective goods following merely the economic rationality of individual self-interest. His theory is intended to explain collective action in the broad sense — not merely that which leads to the formation of nonprofit organizations but equally that which leads to the formation of for-profit organizations and to the formation of the state itself. His model essentially postulates that individuals will make sacrifices to join groups to pursue a collective good depending on the share of that collective good each individual can expect to receive multiplied by a factor roughly corresponding to the probability of the individual sacrifice affecting the provision of the collective good as a whole. Where these conditions do not apply, notably in large groups in which each individual's sacrifice (or contribution) is unlikely to make much difference, he argues that it would not be economically rational for individuals to make the sacrifice or pay the dues to achieve a collective good. In these cases some form of coercion or at least "a separate and selective incentive" must be introduced to stimulate "the rational man to act in a group oriented way." Some commentators imply that Mancur Olson is denying the possibility of genuinely disinterested collective action without compulsion or at least some "separate and selective incentive." This seems to me to be misreading Olson. Although he does not labor the point, he does quite specifically exclude "philanthropic and religious" organizations.[3] It seems to me that his analysis is intended to apply only to the class of nonprofit organization in which the members share in the collective good provided by the organization. There are many such organizations that have adopted the nonprofit form, for example, trade unions and many kinds of professional interest groups. An economic theory that applies to them is no less valuable because it will not apply to the nonprofit organization, the members or benefactors of which do not share in the benefits provided, that I define as genuinely altruistic.

Robert Cameron Mitchell[4] has made an extensive survey of members of national environmental lobbies in order to test Olson's theories. He shows that even when Olson's conditions do not apply, members are in fact prepared to make relatively small personal sacrifices to advance an environmental or social cause with which they identify without any form of compulsion or "separate and selective incentive." From these relatively trivial but widespread instances of philanthropic behavior, we can move through a whole spectrum of altruism ranging from alms given personally or through eleemosynary institutions to the poor at home or in the underdeveloped countries, through communities like that of Mother Teresa in Calcutta of men and women who have accepted poverty to devote their lives to the service of others and ultimately to the heroic examples of those who have laid down their lives for a cause. Departures from the individual rationality of economics are not confined to saintly acts of heroism, environmental concerns, or charitable giving. Patriotism and family loyalty are both powerful social forces that can only rarely be shown to be economically rational. Nor are such departures from individual rationality always necessarily beneficial to society. Trade union loyalty can, for example, occasionally be both irrational from the point of view of the individual member and harmful to society — as when it is forcing wages above the level where there is a demand for the individual member's labor and thus contributing to the phenomenon of "stagflation."

EVOLUTION, ACCULTURATION, AND SOCIALIZATIONAL

Kenneth Arrow[5] notes that actual behavior shows that individuals are in fact willing to make sacrifices for others by making both present sacrifices for future generations and sacrifices for the sick and the poor of the present generation. Quoting Kropotkin and Wynne Edwards, he speculates that there may be some "built-in evolutionary mechanism to this end for altruism aids in the survival of the species." The argument would be that "a group, such as a species or a population within a species, whose individual members are prepared to sacrifice themselves for the welfare of the group, may be less likely to go extinct than a rival group whose individual members place their own selfish interest first." According to Richard Dawkins,[6] this theory of "group selection" is associated with V.C. Wynne-Edwards and Robert Ardrey[7] and was "long assumed to be true by biologists not familiar with the details of evolutionary theory." It is now, according to Dawkins, regarded as unorthodox and is overtaken by the theory of "individual selection."

Dawkins's own theory is curiously reminiscent of the traditional Christian doctrine of original sin — "We are born selfish." The tendency toward selfishness, or, as the theologians would say, "concupiscence," is implanted in us by our genes. If you wish "to build a society in which individuals cooperate generously and unselfishly towards a common good, you can expect little help from biological nature." However, if we understand what our selfish genes are up to, we have a chance to upset their designs, "something which no other species has ever aspired to."

"We have the power to defy the selfish genes of our birth," he writes. The role that the theologians ascribe to "grace" in defying the tendencies of our "fallen nature" Dawkins ascribes to a concept he terms a "meme."[8] This is a social analogue to the biological concept of a gene reproduced not biologically but culturally. "Memes" are ideas, values, and attitudes transmitted over time from generation to generation by processes of acculturation and socialization.

It is difficult to understand how even processes of acculturation and socialization can "help to build a society in which individuals cooperate generously and unselfishly towards a common good" either for the present time or future generations so long as the only rationality we recognize is based on self-interest. What interest is it to me if the human race destroys itself in the generation of my great-grandchildren? Yet there are today literally thousands who demonstrate their anxiety about the possibly cataclysmic consequences to future generations of contemporary problems like the disposal of nuclear wastes. Some of this anxiety may be irrational in the sense of being based on faulty assessments of the risks involved, but we can hardly say that it is irrational to take account of the interest of the people who are not yet born — even though their preference functions cannot, by definition, enter into any current economic or political calculation. As technology extends the time span over which the consequences of current actions can be foreseen, such problems are likely to become of increasing importance and are so seen by vast numbers of people. There are also — and have been throughout history — many who have deliberately sacrificed their own individual good to serve the poor, the sick, and the disabled. To understand the dynamics of these forms of social action, we need some concept wider than individual self-interest.

Adam Smith's concept of sympathy certainly is wide enough. He gives the term an unusually wide definition so that it can refer to almost any circumstances in which we can imagine others to be placed. Those with whom we sympathize in his sense do not necessarily have as yet to be born. We can imagine what it would be like for our great-grandchildren to live in a world polluted by leakages from our nuclear waste disposal sites, and our sympathy with them can prompt us to make present sacrifices. This, indeed, is probably a fairly accurate description of the mental processes that prompt the "no nuke" demonstrators. The trouble with the concept of sympathy is that it is too wide. Charity is more discriminating and does not include every conceivable object with which it is possible to sympathize.

CHRISTIAN DOCTRINE

Adam Smith portrays sympathy as the equivalent precept in nature to the great Christian law of charity, and it is from the Christian doctrine of charity that ultimately most of the law of charities is, in actual historical fact, derived. The law would originally have been administered by the ecclesiastical courts, and it is no coincidence that most of the institutions we still regard as charities by law — universities, schools, hospitals, almhouses, and the like — were originally administered by the church.

The Christian doctrine is probably best first seen in the writings of St. Paul. St. Paul, in his famous description of the virtue of charity, implies an almost total merging of the interests of the individual with those of the collectivity of which he or she is a member. In the Church of Corinth, he was faced with the fairly typical problem of a collectivity riven by doubts, jealousies, and schisms. His principal response[9] was to elaborate the analogy between a collectivity, the church, and a human body. "A man's body is all one although it has a number of different organs and all this multitude of organs goes to make up one body, . . . The eye cannot say to the hand, I have no need of thee (I Corinthians 12:15-21).[10] The diversity is to be prized. After all, "if the whole were one single organ, what would become of the body?" Charity is the unifying force: "God has established a harmony in the body — all the different parts of it were to make each other's welfare their common care" [Ephesians 4:16]. He follows the analogy immediately with the famous description and praise of charity of Chapter Thirteen. The same point, also in relation to the analogy of the body, is made more succinctly in the Letter to the Ephesians: "Thus each limb receiving the active power it needs; it [the body] achieves its natural growth building itself up through charity" (Ephesians 4:16).

St. Paul's argument in these passages totally avoids any reference to self-interest. It does not depend, for example, on any doctrine of compensation in the next world, or on the satisfaction or "psychic rewards" to be derived from serving others or the like. The argument is quite simply that if a community is to perform as an organic whole, its parts must, like the parts of any other organism, merge their lives in mutual interdependence toward a common objective. The implication is clearly that there is something about the dynamics of life in a community that enables the individual members of such a community to view their interest not merely as individuals — but in terms of the community as a whole. It is common experience that members of a family — at least in transactions with those outside the family — frequently view their interests in this way not merely in terms of the individual member's interests but in terms of the interests of the family as a whole. Charity or love is the unifying force within the family, and the family is a powerful symbol of the kind of community that can be built up by charity. Christian charity is a concept that enables the love on which family relations are based to be generalized so as to apply to wider groups.

St. Paul's doctrine of the "mystical body" building itself up by charity is, of course, Christian. The mystical body is the Christian Church whose head is Christ, but charity is not confined to Christianity or even to religion as such. The argument is quite capable of being extended to apply to secular no less than religious institutions, and charity is not peculiar to Christianity. In medieval political theory, the religious and the secular are inextricably intertwined. St. Augustine combines the Pauline doctrine with the Roman law of corporations to form the City of God. This, like Plato's Ideal, is a society situated in heaven of which earthly society exists as a reflection. As Wilks has written,[11] "The juridical person of the Roman *respublica* becomes the mystical person of the Christian society, existing on a heavenly, spiritual level and to be identified with Christ. . . . The juridical reality of the lawyer corresponds to the metaphysical reality of the philosopher and the divine reality of the theologian." The result is highly corporatist.

To quote Wilks again, for the Augustinian

> politically speaking, the well being of one person, ultimately even his existence, is of no account in comparison with the well being of the whole towards which all things are ordered. This produces a real mystique of the political community. The common good of the society is not merely the sum of the individual goods of its members.

Charity in this context is the rule that binds action to the teleological good of the whole of human kind. Unlike Adam Smith's concept of sympathy, this concept of charity does give us a criterion for judging what is and what is not charitable. The criterion is the ultimate good of the community. What it does not tell us is what is the ultimate good or how to choose between different views of the ultimate good. Medieval corporatist theory, like other corporatist theories, really had to assume that the ultimate good of mankind was both one and knowable. Applying such a theory to temporal political institutions presents major problems.

Dawkins's theory of the meme, echoing as it does the biological theory of evolution based on the survival of the fittest genes, does suggest one criterion for judging the ultimate good of temporal societies. Those societies whose culture reproduces and transmits attitudes and values that fit the society to avoid the dangers and hazards presented by its environment will thrive, and the societies that transmit attitudes and values that make it unfit for survival will die out. The mechanism is quite different in biological evolution. Genes are determined by biochemical processes and transmitted biologically. Values and attitudes are consciously determined and transmitted by sociological processes. There is relatively little we can do to change our genes. There is quite a lot we can do to change our attitudes and values. The scope for teleological thinking about values and attitudes is far greater than is the scope for teleological thinking about genetics. But in neither case do we know enough about what the future will hold to be able to say with any confidence which attitudes and values will ultimately prove conducive to the survival of our society — any more than we now know which genes have the highest survival value. Probably all we can learn from the analogy with biological evolution is the value of diversity.

In later chapters I will discuss some of the problems in determining the good for society and how the existence of private voluntary organizations enables some of these problems to be circumvented. However, we have now reached the stage at which we can begin to assess the adequacy of the economic theory of market failure as a rationale for withdrawing transactions from the for-profit sector of market operations and moving them into the nonprofit sectors of government or private voluntary action.

CRITICISMS OF THE MARKET FAILURE RATIONALE

Does the theory of market failure, that is, the definition of the conditions under which markets cannot achieve a Pareto optimum, provide an adequate rationale for nonprofit operations? Because it is limited to the notion of self-interest, it can cast light on the motives of individuals only in a limited class of cases — those in which the individuals are seeking their own gain under conditions when their gain is inseparable from that of others. It can tell us nothing about motives where individuals are acting for the benefit of others without themselves benefiting from their actions. Nor is it only altruistic *motives* that it cannot explain. Because Pareto's concept of efficiency is based on self-regarding preferences without making interpersonal comparisons, the theory cannot even provide a case for altruism, a case for the individual making sacrifices for the benefit of others without being in his or her own view adequately compensated for those sacrifices. The theory is silent as to why the fortunate should make sacrifices for the unfortunate, the rich for the poor, the present generation for future generations, and so forth. Since a great deal not only of voluntary activity but of state activity as well is concerned with encouraging or compelling such behavior, this is a serious limitation. Of course, the theory does not make a case *against* such behavior, for example, suggesting that it is wrong for the wealthy to succor the poor. It merely has to rely on something else, such as some theory of distributive justice, to make the case.

The market failure rationale thus clearly does not provide us with a sufficient definition. But does it provide us with a necessary definition? Can we say that where there is market failure there is always a case for nonprofit operations?

In the case of pure public goods such as national defense, where it is impossible to conceive of any possible means of making such goods the subject of *quid pro quo* transactions, the answer seem to be "yes," insofar as there is any demand for the good in question. In the much more common case of transactions with externalities, the answer is not so clear.

The economic concept of positive externalities is admittedly somewhat more discriminating than is the legal concept of public benefit. A committee under the chairmanship of Lord Goodman, established to review the English law of charities, argued that public benefit is not a sufficient definition of charity. They argue that a successful commercial venture providing massive new employment opportunities is manifestly of immense benefit to the entire community in which it is located, and an indefinite number of people will indirectly benefit from its activities.[12] Yet no one would think of classifying it as anything other than a market operation. The welfare economist can distinguish this case. He can point out that the Goodman Committee's hypothetical commercial venture will not necessarily produce externalities. It will not do so if conditions of perfect competition and, in particular, if conditions of full employment apply.

Conversely, the existence of positive externalities will not always be sufficient to bring a transaction within the definition of charity. James Meade,[11] for example, gives, as an illustration of externalities, the benefits that may be reaped by a beekeeper from the orchard maintained by a neighboring fruit grower. The same argument will apply to the benefit derived by the fruit grower from the bees pollinating his or her apple trees, and, in fact, this externality of beekeeping is often captured by the fruit grower paying the beekeeper to establish his or her hives in his or her orchard. We can avoid this complication by accepting, for the purposes of the argument, only those externalities that benefit an indeterminable number of beneficiaries. Justice Gray,[13] as long ago as 1867, emphasized that to be categorized as charitable a gift must benefit "an indefinite number of persons." But to say that the beneficiaries must be an indefinite number is not sufficient. For an activity to be regarded as charitable and thus a proper member of the Third Sector under this head, the form of benefit must be defined. Justice Gray defined the way the indefinite number could be benefited as "either by bringing their minds and hearts under the influence of education, religion, by relieving their bodies from disease, suffering or constraint, by assisting them to establishing themselves in life, or by erecting or maintaining public buildings or works or otherwise lessening the burdens of government." We can add a few more categories as the concept of charity has evolved since 1867 — e.g., the prevention of cruelty to animals.

If we limit ourselves to positive externalities from which an indefinite number of unidentifiable persons benefit, have we succeeded in stating the conditions that the common law would recognize as charitable? Surely not. To take a frivolous example. Most of us — or at least most of the males among us — will derive considerable pleasure from seeing well-dressed women walking about the streets. This is a benefit that cannot be appropriated by the dressmaker. Anyone who has seen the film *My Fair Lady* would have noticed what a remarkable public spectacle was provided, in Edwardian days, by such events as the Ascot Racemeeting, which the fashionable attended in all their finery. Yet even if one could imagine dressmaking being carried on as a nonprofit activity, no one would seriously suggest that providing dresses for the richer sections of society should be classed as charitable and exempted from taxation on the grounds that an indefinite number of persons derived benefit from watching its products. Clearly a social judgment is involved in determining what is a charitable activity that involves other criteria than the economic criterion of externalities.

This objection applies more generally than this frivolous example may suggest. Crucial to the concept of Pareto optimality is the assumption of perfect competition, and wherever this assumption does not apply, there will be externalities, either positive or negative. We know that, in practice, there are wide areas of industry and commerce in which all the assumptions of perfect competition do not apply.

The economic concept of externalities, like the legal concept of public benefit, is much too wide. Remember that a case for going outside the disciplines of the market can, according to this theory, be made whether the externalities are positive or negative, and with very little ingenuity almost any transaction can be shown to have positive or negative externalities. Pushed to its logical conclusion, the market failure argument can be used to justify government intervention or nonprofit operation in almost any circumstances.

The market failure argument, or more precisely the concept of Pareto optimality, will not in all cases identify the conditions under which free markets will fail to result in a distribution of resources that a caring society will consider satisfactory because it is caught by the limitations of the paradigm of self-interest. Conversely, even within these limitations, the test of market failure is too crude to distinguish between those cases where common sense suggests the distribution of resources can be left to market forces and those cases where common sense suggests that it cannot. There is also a third limitation to the market failure rationale. Even where the concept of market failure provides an economic justification for nonmarket operations, it can do no more than provide a *prima facie* case as to where intervention should take place; it cannot tell us how much intervention is needed.

At first sight, the concepts of market failure and Pareto optimality do seem to promise to be able to answer the question of "how much" intervention is required. Let us this time take the illustration of a negative externality, say, air pollution produced by a steel works. The market failure argument suggests that this steel works would produce too much steel compared to the Pareto optimum, which would be the economic level of production if the costs of pollution were recoverable from the steel works. At first sight, therefore, it would seem that there is a clear, quantitative criterion for government intervention; the government should intervene (by taxation, regulation, or other appropriate means) just so much as to reduce production to the Pareto optimum level, neither more nor less. However, the situation of market failure arose in the first place precisely because pollution was a "bad" to which no price could be attached. If a price could have been attached, there would have been no market failure, and all that would have been required is a method by which those who had suffered the harmful effects could charge the price to the producer.

There are two aspects to this failure of the market. Those who suffer the harmful effects are not parties to the transaction and hence their views could not affect the decision. But also because they are not parties to any exchange transaction, they are in no position to express the cost to themselves in terms to which the market can react. The market transactions on which Pareto relied to achieve his state of maximum efficiency are real, actual choices made by those affected by a transaction. The government officials who have to judge the degree of intervention that is desirable cannot use any measure based on preferences in situations of actual choice by those affected. All the government officials can do is to make a political judgment as to where balance between the cost and the benefits to the community lies. This will vary widely according to the assumptions.[14]

The argument is, of course, the same if we take a positive externality or a public good as our illustration and reverse the signs throughout. Moreover, because we cannot tell by how much government or other nonprofits should intervene, we can never be absolutely certain that the intervention has done more good than harm. William Niskanen,[15] in fact, argues that output produced by a bureaucratic system will necessarily exceed the output that would have been produced by competitive industry faced by the same demand and cost conditions, and hence, represents a maldistribution of resources. Assuming that the typical product produced by a government agency or a private nonprofit is a public good, I find this argument difficult to accept. The theory of market failure will tell us only that producers subject to market forces alone will tend to produce less of the public good than the Pareto optimum, but it cannot tell us how much production needs to be increased and cannot say when there will be too much. Market economics cannot, for example, tell us how much national defense should be produced. This can be only a political judgment. Like Burton Weisbrod,[16] I would maintain that supply by government or by private nonprofits may on occasion be excessive and on other occasions be inadequate. An illustration of a service provided as a public good that intuitively appears to be inadequate rather than excessive would be the British National Health Service.[17] On the other hand, it is often argued that little-used country roads in England and Scotland are maintained to an unnecessarily high standard and thus would represent the sort of maldistribution of resources Niskanen claims to be a general characteristic of all public sector supply.

The characteristic of all externalities, whether we are thinking of pure public goods like clean air or services having positive externalities like education, public health, and the arts, is that they are seen as possessing a value beyond that which is or, in many cases can be, expressed by price. However, the increment of value over price is indeterminate and will vary according to the eye of the beholder. Thus the problem we noticed with eleemosynary charities — that there could be no Pareto optimum for the redistribution of wealth — applies wherever externalities occur. In these latter cases a Pareto optimum may be hypothetically conceivable, but its position is in practice unknowable. It could be known only if the service in question were moved into the market sector — as, for example, when common land was made private property and the costs of grazing it subject to the market discipline of price. What this implies for the roles of government and voluntary nonprofit organizations in establishing social values is a question to which I will return, but first I review an important variant of the externalities or market failure argument that is based on the concept of trust.

6

Failure of Trust in the Market

Although market economics presupposes that the parties to a transaction will be motivated by self-interest, trust in the supplier of goods and services is quite necessary to the operation of the system. This has been recognized since at least the nineteenth century. In Britain, this recognition received statutory expression in the Sale of Goods Act of 1893.[1] Two provisions of that Act show how seriously the Victorians took the responsibilities of shopkeepers. Where a buyer expressly or implicitly "relies on the seller's skill or judgment and the goods are of a description which it is in the course of the seller's business to supply," there is an implied condition that the goods should be "reasonably fit for such purpose." Similarly, when goods are bought by description from a seller who deals in goods of that description, there is an implied condition that the goods are of "merchantable quality." Merchantable quality means that the article is of such quality and in such condition that a reasonable individual acting reasonably would, after full examination, accept it in performance of his or her offer to buy it.

Two cases brought under the Act demonstrate that the consequence of uninformed choice in even quite trivial purchases may be exceedingly serious. In one case,[2] a shopkeeper had sold a bottle of mineral water; the bottle subsequently burst, injuring the plaintiff. The shopkeeper was held liable for the injury caused to the plaintiff. In another case,[3] a child had bought a six-penny catapult. The catapult was defective and broke when the child tried to use it. The stone flew up and hit the child's eye, damaging it irremediably. The defendants were held liable for the loss of the child's eye and had to pay considerable damages.

The Victorian legislators were remarkably clear-sighted about the respects in which, in even the most trivial of transactions, the buyer is dependent on the trustworthiness of the seller.[4] Suspicion that those who operate in a for-profit environment cannot be trusted is, however, quite widespread. Some radical thinkers have even argued that the profit-seeking discipline undermines moral values.

In the United Kingdom, blood donors are never paid and must be presumed, therefore, to be motivated by altruism. In the United States, a significant proportion of blood for transfusion comes from paid donors. Richard Titmuss uses this distinction, in *The Gift Relationship,* almost as a parable, to contrast the "ethics of the marketplace" with the social values of a system based on altruism. He amasses an extraordinary collection of data designed to show the superiority of the "voluntary system" over the "commercialized blood market." The commercial system is wasteful, inefficient, and unethical: Donors are exploited, the product is far more costly, more of it gets wasted, and, in terms of quality, the commercial market is much more likely to distribute contaminated blood. Under the commercial system, everybody and everything — donors, recipients, doctors, society, science, and medical ethics — all suffer, according to Titmuss. More generally, he argues that the very existence of a commercial market tends to replace and destroy communal values while, conversely, the institutions of the welfare state, such as the National Health Service, mold people's values towards the ideal of generosity of which the impersonal gift of blood is a fitting symbol.[5]

In reviewing the book, Kenneth Arrow,[6] while rejecting Titmuss's more extravagant claims, focuses on the best-documented case. This is the much greater probability of commercial blood being contaminated. The fact is well documented on both sides of the Atlantic and established with good experimental evidence. Moreover, in this case, Titmuss can go beyond his usual *post hoc propter hoc* argument and suggest a theory linking cause and effect. The most common contaminant of human blood in the United Kingdom and the United States is the virus of *serum hepatitis* and, apparently, there is no means of discovering its existence except for the trustworthiness of donors in declaring that they suffer from the disease. A voluntary donor wishing to make a "good gift" of life-saving and not potentially lethal blood has no incentive to hide his or her infection. The paid donors, on the other hand — particularly, we are told, those from prisons and skid row populations — have every incentive to do so. Arrow comments that the situation has parallels wherever there is uncertainty about the quality of a service or commodity and a difference between the degrees of knowledge possessed by supplier and consumer. He suggests that "the supplying of truthful information is an example of an externality," thus linking this form of market failure to that which we have already considered.

Arrow does not himself suggest that this form of market failure is necessarily corrected by the intervention of non-profit organizations. Indeed, the example he gives of another commodity in which the same situation applies, an automobile about whose safety the supplier would be better informed than the purchaser, is clearly drawn from the market sector and would be subject to correction by government regulation. The implication of Arrow's argument is, rather, that apart from the very special case of altruistically supplied blood, where the situation is self-enforcing, the appropriate corrective is regulation, as in the case of the negative externality of air pollution.

In studying another case in which nonprofit operations are common, the day care of young children, Richard Nelson and Michael Krashinsky,[7] note the "near consensus . . . that private for profit enterprises and the market represent an unsatisfactory way of organizing the activity." Seeking to explain this in a country in which private enterprise solutions tend to be exalted, they note two characteristics that closely parallel the two picked out by Arrow from the Titmuss study: uncertainty about the quality of the service provided and the lack of adequate ability to evaluate it on the part of the consumers — the children or their parents. To this they add a third that could be applied to the blood transfusion case or, for that matter, to the case of the doubtfully safe automobile — "that the costs of uninformed choice may be very serious."

Nelson and Krashinsky go on to consider, in the case of day care, the third alternative: public supply by the government sector. They recognize that there are both private and public interests in the service, that is to say, in the language that we have been using so far, that the service is partly a public good with positive externalities. However, public supply would be likely to result in a public monopoly, which, in the case of day care, seems undesirable. The consumer's lack of expertise and possible bias — parents considering their own convenience rather than the good of the children — suggests the need for something more than consumer choice. On the other hand, there is not sufficient knowledge about what is really good child care to be able to maintain that professional judgment alone is a sufficient safeguard. What is required is a blend of consumer sovereignty and professional judgment. The market enables consumers to exercise judgment by changing supplier.

Albert Hirschman (in *Exit Voice and Loyalty)* called this way of influencing suppliers "exit" (the customer *leaves* his or her supplier even if he or she joins another). Hirschman argues that traditional economics has tended to neglect another method of influencing suppliers, which he called "voice," by the customer complaining to the supplier to whom in other respects he or she remains loyal. Exit is not very satisfactory in the case of day care, if only because it cannot be good for children to be moved about from one center to another until the parents find a satisfactory one. On the other hand, Hirschman's alternative, "voice," is not wholly satisfactory either. Needs and tastes differ. Controls and collective decisions by a group with diverse preferences present difficulties, some of which I will consider later. Therefore, both "exit" and "voice" must be given due weight as control devices. As Nelson and Krashinsky conclude, this analysis is not peculiar to the case of day care for young children. Very similar issues will apply to a wide range of goods and services such as medical care, education, legal services, care for the elderly, public transport, and many local and competitive public goods.

Henry Hansmann[8] faces the challenge of applying trust as a rationale for the whole of the nonprofit sector. In fact, he takes an even broader view of the nonprofit sector than I do, as I have tended to concentrate on the charitable subset of nonprofit organizations. These, in general, are those which in the United States are tax exempt under Section 501(c)(3). It is interesting to note that the Californian Nonprofit Corporation Law draws a sharp distinction between what are termed "mutual benefit" corporations and "public benefit" corporations. The latter corresponds quite closely to the charitable subset.

Ira Ellman makes a strong case for regarding these as two quite different categories of nonprofit corporations,[9] with mutual benefit corporations being in many ways closer to commercial corporations. Yet, in reality, we are probably dealing here, as so often within this field, with a seamless web. It would be absurd to exclude from membership of a public benefit corporation, say, a charity to help the disabled, people who were capable of benefiting from its activities, say, people themselves disabled. At the same time, the activities of mutual benefit corporations may very often benefit a wider public than their members. For example, the activities of the American Automobile Association will presumably in many cases benefit motorists generally whether or not they are members. Hansmann therefore seems to me to be quite entitled to seek a rationale that will go to the heart of the whole distinction between for profit and nonprofit operation. He expresses the crux of his argument succinctly:

> Occasionally, due either to the circumstances under which the product is purchased and consumed or to the nature of the product itself, consumers may be incapable of evaluating with any accuracy the goods promised or delivered. . . . In situations of this type, consumers might find themselves considerably better off if they deal with non-profit producers rather than with for-profit producers. While the non-profit producer, like its for-profit counterpart may have the capacity to raise prices and cut quality in such cases without fear of customer reprisal, it has nowhere near the same incentive since those in charge are barred from taking home the profit. . . . In essence [this line of reasoning] is saying nothing more than that we can view all non-profits in very much the same way that we have always viewed charitable trusts — that is to say as fiduciaries.[10]

Hansmann then applies this line of argument to a whole range of illustrations organized under a fourfold classification of nonprofit organizations. His most elegant illustration is probably the first: the application to eleemosynary institutions. Eleemosynary institutions, by definition, distribute alms, that is to say, nonreciprocal gifts — where, in current practice, the ultimate beneficiary is unlikely to be known to the original donor. He takes CARE as an illustration of such an eleemosynary institution. CARE gets nearly all its funds from contributors in the developed world and distributes them to the needy perhaps half the world away from the original contributor. The original contributor has virtually no connection with the ultimate beneficiary. A contribution to CARE is giving almost as impersonal a gift as Titmuss's gift of blood. Precisely for this reason the original contributor or customer must rely entirely on the trustworthiness of CARE to ensure that they do what they said they would do with his money.

> If CARE were organized for-profit, it would have a strong incentive to skimp badly on the services it promises, or even neglect to perform them entirely, and divert most or all of its income directly to its owners. After all, few of its customers could be expected to travel to India or Africa to see if the food they paid for was in fact ever delivered, much less delivered as, when, and where specified. . . . For the services of the type that CARE provides, then, it stands to reason that an individual would want to deal only with a non-profit firm, since in that case he has the additional protection provided by the non-distribution constraint.[11]

He applies the same argument to other cases where the person paying for the goods or services is different from the persons receiving that service — for example, children's day care, schooling, or nursing homes. In these cases the parent paying for the child or the child paying for the parent must to a greater extent than in the normal market transaction trust the supplier to deliver what he or she promises. Hansmann also applies the same argument where the beneficiary cannot be identified: for example, radio and other public goods. By a slight extension of the concept of trust, he also applies it to hospitals (where patients are really in no position to judge whether the service they are getting is either necessary or good) and even to contributions to the opera and other performing arts. "Since there will be no observable connection between the individual's contribution and the quality of the performance seen, he needs the non-profit constraint to assure him that in fact his contribution is being used to meet the costs of the firm's productions."[12]

Hansmann decorates this basic theme with subsidary arguments that are often insightful but occasionally overingenious. In the case of alumni contributions to private colleges and universities, the contributor needs the nonprofit constraint to be sure that his or her contribution is used to further the educational goals of the institution rather than lining someone's pocket. Hansmann also develops a subtle argument that such contributions are, in effect, voluntary repayment for the benefit the alumnus received from his or her school or university education, "something like a loan program with a voluntary payback."[13] One is left wondering, if this is merely a reciprocal deal, if the contribution is only a deferred *quid* for a *quo* previously received, why such contributions should be tax deductible and the institutions tax exempt. Certainly, we can accept that loyalty and gratitude play a part in alumni contributions and that there is thus an element of reciprocity about the gift. Private schools and universities may not be wholly eleemosynary institutions, but the advancement of education has been recognized as a charitable purpose for the best part of a thousand years.

In discussing exclusive social clubs, Hansmann advances an ingenious argument that the nonprofit form is preferred in these cases because, were they organized for profit, the owners would be in a position to make a monopoly profit out of the members' own high social status. Certainly, my own very limited experience of exclusive social clubs suggests that the nonprofit form *is* usually preferred. The only exceptions that come readily to mind are gambling clubs. But I suspect that the true explanation is that only gambling clubs offer the prospect of a commercially adequate return on the assets involved.

Hansmann does not, of course, suggest that these subsidiary arguments are necessarily connected to the notion of trust. The fact that he uses more than one form of argument suggests that he feels that all forms of nonprofit organization cannot be explained by a single rationale, and in this I am sure that he is right.

Does the market failure argument that is based on the concept of trust take us any further than that based on the more general concept of externalities? Undoubtedly there is a certain elegance in an economic analysis that brings us back to the Anglo-Saxon common law tradition of charities. The weaknesses we found with the form of the argument based on externalities were that it provided neither a sufficient nor a necessary definition. It covered both too much and too little: too much because almost every transaction can be shown to produce some sort of externality; too little because it can explain neither the motive nor the need for genuinely altruistic behavior. Does "trust" work any better? Certainly there is a sense in which trust is so pervasive a requisite that it must be a necessary condition in every social relationship. Certainly the benefactor who establishes an endowment for the relief of poverty must be able to trust the trustees he or she appoints. But does "trust" help us to understand *why* he or she does it or why it is *good* that he or she should do it? I think not. Probably there is no rational explanation for altruism other than the ultimately mysterious way in which humans feel that they are "members one of another," whether, like Adam Smith, we attribute this to imagination, which enables us to feel sympathy or, like St. Paul, to the God-given gift of love.

Conversely the "trust form" is at least as open as the "externalities form" to the objection that it covers too much.

I have little difficulty in accepting that in all transactions with nonprofit organizations, the contributor has to rely heavily on the trustworthiness of the organization. My difficulty is rather that this does not seem to me a sufficiently distinctive characteristic to identify the role of the nonprofit enterprise.

Arrow, in the article quoted above, suggests that a greater measure of trustworthiness than the market can be relied on to provide will be needed wherever the supplier is better informed than the consumer. He gives the example of the safety of an automobile, which will obviously be better known to the seller than to the buyer, but we do not normally buy second-hand cars from nonprofit organizations. When we consider transactions involving even greater skill and judgment on the part of the supplier, the need for trust in the supplier becomes even greater. The argument would suggest that in fields in which great skill and judgment are required of the supplier and in which there is a great discrepancy between the knowledge possessed by the supplier and that of the consumer, we would find a proliferation of nonprofit organizations. Yet this does not happen. Private medical practice, dentistry, the law, the learned professions generally, the manufacture of pharmaceutical drugs, electrical contracting, any number of building trade crafts, and automobile and television repairs are all fields in which the for-profit form is dominant.

Hansmann does endeavor to deal with this difficulty. He points out that in most of these cases, consumers have other forms of protection. Doctors and lawyers have to be licensed and are subject to supervision by their respective professional bodies. Drugs are subject to federal regulation. Plumbers and electricians in many states have to be licensed. Where there is no such licensing or regulation, as for example in the case of television and automobile repairs, we must assume that consumers are not overly concerned about their inability to judge the quality of the service.

Hansmann's argument, at this point, is no longer an argument based strictly on market failure but rather on the presence or absence of other forms of protection for the consumer usually provided by the government sector. One might almost be tempted to say that it is an argument based on government failure rather than market failure but for the fact that the presence or absence of governmental supervision does not distinguish the nonprofit from the commercial sectors. Many nonprofit organizations — schools, hospitals, and universities — are subject to supervision and some measure of control by the public authorities. Rightly so, for abuses are not unknown in the nonprofit sector.

Hansmann finds it necessary to look for other characteristics of the transaction. Of these the most significant, in my view, is the difference in the importance and the time span of the transaction. The consumer purchasing drugs or the services of the repairperson can switch relatively easily from one supplier to another, but the parents of a child enrolled in a day care center or a school may be reluctant to uproot the child and send him or her someplace else. Similarly, old people may find that changing nursing homes in is a much more difficult decision than changing the brand of cereals they have for breakfast. Translating this point into Hirschman's language, Hansmann suggests that transactions with nonprofit organizations are frequently of a kind in which "exit" is likely to be an ineffective safeguard and in which in consequence the consumer has to an unusual extent to rely on "voice."

Ira Ellman[14] makes essentially the same point. Patients in a nursing home will, all too often, find that the threat of leaving is no more than an empty threat. All they can do is complain and trust that there is something about the way the nursing home is organized that is likely to make their complaints more effective than they would be in a for-profit enterprise. "We may wish to consider," he writes, "whether membership in a non-profit corporation, when chosen over an alternative of purchasing goods or services in the profit sector, involves the members' sacrifice of 'exit' mobility in the expectation of greater 'voice,' thus possibly justifying increased assurances of member democracy." Certainly a desire to gain "voice," ultimately a political motive, often seems to be the motive for membership in a nonprofit organization.

This suggests that it is in the political sphere broadly interpreted, rather than in conventional economics, that we will find the true rationale for nonprofit organizations. Yet even this distinction does not fully distinguish the fields in which nonprofits are common from those in which they are not. Some market transactions do represent important long-term decisions from which "exit" is difficult — for example, the decision to buy or build a house. Conversely, contributions to nonprofit charities may be spontaneous transitory decisions carrying very little "voice." (However, we should note that even such spontaneous contributions are an inarticulate expression of support for the objectives of the charity concerned. When we place a quarter in the plate brought round by the Salvation Army lady, we are casting a silent vote for the objectives of the Salvation Army.)

Beyond these arguments, Hansmann suggests that there may be reasons rooted in cultural norms that lead individuals to prefer the nonprofit form more in some cases than in others. Can we identify these reasons from which the cultural norms spring? I think that in many cases we can, and the clue lies in the first of the characteristics that Nelson and Krashinsky identified in the day care case — that is, that there are both private and public interests in the good or service involved. In other words, day care has a value that cannot be wholly judged on its price. There are social benefits, or positive externalities, in the service. This brings us back to the earlier version of the market failure argument — that based on public goods, or positive externalities.

7

The Nonprofit Sector as an Alternative to Government and the Categorical Constraint

So far we have been concerned with nonprofit organizations as alternatives to for-profit or commercial sector organizations. The market failure rationale with which we have been dealing is essentially a logical or analytic exercise that identifies the conditions under which for-profit operations will lead to a misallocation of resources under the normal assumptions of market economics. It is not a very satisfactory rationale in part because these conditions occur so often (or can be argued to occur so often) in the real world that a case for nonprofit operations can be made in relation to almost anything.

In the industrialized countries of the West, we have, of course, seen throughout the greater part of the century a tendency to remove transactions from the unfettered operations of market forces and to extend both government regulation and the supply of goods and services by government. Without necessarily believing that these tendencies are wholly pernicious, we can easily see that the market failure argument in the simple form in which I have dealt with it in this book could very well lead us to suppress all free enterprise in the name of correcting market failure. The more sophisticated form of the argument in which the relative advantages of conducting affairs through the alternatives of the market, the government, or voluntary agencies are balanced against each other, in terms of "transaction costs," would enable us to be more discriminating. Yet even the language of transaction costs would not provide us with a genuinely objective criterion for ascribing affairs to one or another of the three sectors because the "costs" in question are frequently unquantifiable and a reflection of fundamental values that transcend the values on which a price can be put by conventional economics. The economic cost (in the narrow sense) of enclosing the common land was, for example, negligible; the true cost, which almost certainly today we would have found unbearable, was the human misery it created. This certainly is not measurable without interpersonal comparisons of utility.

The market failure rationale nonetheless gives us some help in defining the commercial for-profit sector and the nonprofit sectors. But it will not help us define the boundary — in many ways the more important boundary — between the private nonprofit sector and the government sector, since both are nonprofit. Moreover, we need, in practice, a third boundary separating nonprofit organizations from the personal sector, in which individuals allocate resources within their own household.

Somewhat over a hundred years ago, Alexis de Tocqueville had begun to sketch out these three boundaries in his classic *Democracy in America*. In a much quoted passage he wrote:

> Americans of all ages, all conditions, and all dispositions constantly form associations. They have not only com-

> mercial and manufacturing companies, in which all take part, but associations of a thousand other kinds, religious, moral, serious, futile, general or restricted, enormous or diminutive. The Americans make associations to give entertainments, to found seminaries, to build inns, to construct churches, to diffuse books, to send missionaries to the antipodes; in this manner they found hospitals, prisons and schools. . . . Wherever at the head of some new undertaking you see the government in France, or a man of rank in England, in the United States you will be sure to find an association.[1]

Curiously enough, Tocqueville, unlike latter-day economists, was not greatly concerned with distinguishing nonprofit organizations from for-profit enterprises. The term he uses, "public associations," covers both. He is primarily concerned with distinguishing among what he sees as the characteristically American way of proceeding by way of voluntary associations from, on the one hand, the method of proceeding by way of a government agency, which he sees as characteristically French, and, on the other, from what he sees as the characteristically English way of "performing great things singly." He traces the American tendency to form associations to the American concept of democracy, which he sees both as a system of government and as an egalitarian society.

In the aristocratic England of his time, there was less need for voluntary associations, and individuals could achieve great things single-handedly.

> In aristocratic society, men do not need to combine in order to act, because they are strongly held together. Every wealthy and powerful citizen constitutes the head of a permanent and compulsory association, composed of all those who are dependent upon him, or whom he makes subservient to the execution of his design. Amongst democratic nations, on the contrary [and by this he appears to

> mean in egalitarian societies], all the citizens are independent and feeble; they can do hardly anything by themselves, and none of them can oblige his fellowmen to lend him their assistance. They all therefore become powerless, if they do not learn voluntarily to help each other.[2]

The French, on the other hand — and again we should remember that he is writing in the first half of the nineteenth century — tend to believe that an able and active government ought to execute for society at large what individuals can no longer accomplish individually. He believes this approach to be mistaken. As industrialization proceeded, he foresaw that the scope for the economically self-sufficient individual would ever diminish and the tasks of government would proliferate beyond the powers of government adequately to perform. Moreover, society needs to create "fresh feelings and fresh opinions." A government "can only dictate strict rules" and rigidly enforce the opinions it favors.

> A government can no more be competent to keep alive and to renew the circulation of opinions and feelings among a great people, than to manage all the speculations of productive industry. . . . Government should not be the only active power; associations ought, in democratic nations, to stand in lieu of those powerful private individuals whom the equality of conditions has swept away.[3]

I do not propose to elaborate on Tocqueville's distinction of voluntary associations for individual action. His argument is sufficient. Today we do not need much persuading that individuals can rarely achieve great things in our complex society without the collaboration of others. We are more concerned about how that collaboration should be structured, whether by the incentive of profit, the compulsion of law, or the impulse of generosity. The great oligarchs of eighteenth-century England, from whom Tocqueville felt it necessary to distinguish the voluntary American associations, have, for all intents and purposes, disappeared into history. Insofar as any survive as their successors, we find them today not as a separate sector of the political economy but within the commercial voluntary sectors. Indeed, their role, which Tocqueville saw as a safeguard against the danger of an overmighty government, is to a great extent in contemporary America played by the big foundations that were established after his time by an industrial and commercial aristocracy whose emergence he did not foresee.

Tocqueville's argument that voluntary associations (or "private philanthropy") are an alternative to government, in some ways a preferable alternative, is, by contrast, as relevant today as in the 1830s. Much the same point is made in the 1970s by Jane Mavity and Paul Ylvisaker. In a paper for the Filer Commission, they wrote:

> The giving part of philanthropy (foundations, corporations and individuals) carr[ies] on privately a function that is essentially the counterpart of what is done by the public legislatures: they "listen" to public opinion, identify social problems, frame the issues, choose ways of dealing with those issues, resolve at least to their own satisfaction the competing claims of supplicants and advisors, assemble financial resources, appropriate money, and then evaluate performance.
>
> The distinctive attributes of this private legislative process are that it can intervene in public matters without having to levy taxes or get elected; that it acts by persuasion and contract, not by force of law; and that it is ultimately subordinate, or at least accountable, to the public legislative process.
>
> The spending and doing side of philanthropy — the thousands of agencies through which money is donated and through which it is then dispensed — similarly has its public analogue in the administrative agencies of government.[4]

WHEN GOVERNMENT IS THE ALTERNATIVE TO BE PREFERRED

However, if government and private philanthropy are alternatives, when should we prefer the one and when the other? First, we can see that there are cases when government action is, in practice, the only feasible alternative. Returning to the market failure argument, it is, for example, virtually impossible to see how a negative externality, such as air pollution, could be corrected by voluntary action alone. Private nonprofits can supplement the commercial sector in the case of positive externalities where market producers are liable to produce too little, but in the case of negative externalities, private nonprofits cannot collect from the producer the unchargeable costs. In such cases, the agency of government and coercion is necessary to tax, or to regulate, the damage that cannot be compensated through free-market transactions. A private nonprofit can, in these cases, provide only the public good of representing the case for such regulation — at the same time as other nonprofits may be providing the complementary and opposite case against undue regulation. Very occasionally private nonprofits can also assist in the enforcement of the law, as happens when some environmental protection society helps to enforce, say, the laws against pollution. But such cases are relatively rare.

Second, there are cases where merely organizing an activity on a private nonprofit basis will not provide sufficient safeguards of the public interest. This seems to be the case of the so-called natural monopolies, such as the provision of utilities — water, gas, electricity, railways, telephones, and the like. Occasionally such utilities are provided by private nonprofit cooperatives, but even when this is the case, the nonprofit cooperative is subjected to very much the same system of regulations as is a for-profit enterprise. Public sector action seems almost invariably to be required in such cases. The public sector action may take the form of government regulation or it may take the form of public sector provision by a nationalized enterprise. The historic trend seems to run from regulation to public provision. In Britain, for example, gas, electricity, and railways were originally provided by privately owned but publicly regulated enterprises, but these were nationalized after World War II. In the United States, the publicly regulated private sector undertakings have survived somewhat longer but, even here, Amtrak and Conrail mark a tendency toward the nationalization of rail transport.

Third, there are cases where private nonprofit organizations appear to be incapable of mobilizing sufficient resources to meet the demands of most citizens, and the compulsive power of government has to be invoked to coerce payment of the cost through taxation. This situation can arise because of the free rider problem. Although many people want the service to be provided, few of them are prepared voluntarily to make the necessary sacrifices and bear the costs without being coerced, because, as Mancur Olson would argue, the link is too tenuous between their contributions and the scale on which the service is provided. There are clearly considerable problems in deciding how much people are prepared to pay for the provision of a service that they cannot buy in the ordinary way as a *quid pro quo* transaction. Ultimately, resolving these problems is a task for political judgment. However, an elegant economic analysis by Burton Weisbrod both helps us understand the problem better and explains why the activities of government may frequently need to be supplemented by the voluntary activities of nonprofit organizations.

Weisbrod's Model

To follow Weisbrod's[5] argument, let me first recapitulate the public goods rationale described in Chapter 4. There is a whole range of things that an indefinite number of us want to a greater or lesser degree. These may be things we want because we want to use them ourselves (bridges and highways) or because we think the country ought to have them (national defense, schools, hospitals, social services). But in either case, what these goods have in common is that we cannot pay for them in the usual way of going into a shop to buy them. The things we want for our country we fairly obviously cannot buy in the usual market or shopping way, and the things we want for our own use are things for which, for one reason or another, unit pricing is either impractical or too costly.

So far, the argument appears to point invariably to government as the source of supply, but this is because so far the argument has assumed implicitly that all citizens' wants are the same. If all citizens did want the same and to the same degree — and also, of course, if we could determine how much of any public good all citizens wanted — the case for public supply of such goods would be unanswerable. If public-spirited citizens voluntarily supplied a certain output of the public good wanted by all citizens, the less public spirited would be able to take a free ride on the backs of their more public spirited fellow citizens. Unless we made some improbable assumptions about how public spirited people actually are, the total supply of that good would fall short of the level desired by all citizens. Considerations of both justice and economic inefficiency would lead us to say that the government must intervene and compel all citizens (presumably through the tax system) to pay for the goods they all want — remembering that the goods in question are, by definition, goods that cannot be bought in market transactions. But, of course, the assumption that all citizens want the same things to the same extent is manifestly untrue.

This is the point at which Burton Weisbrod starts, in a seminal paper in which occurs the first published reference I have been able to trace to the concept of "a government market failure analogous to the conditions causing private market failures." He assumes, which is surely correct, that different citizens will want public goods to varying extents or, in the language of economics, they will have different demand functions for public goods. He also assumes that public goods may be provided either by government, by private nonprofit organizations, or even by commercial enterprises — when the demand for a public good (such as clean air) may be met by private good substitutes (such as air filters). Leaving aside this last complication, how does government decide how much of a public good to produce?

Weisbrod assumes that for each level of output there is a corresponding level of costs to be paid in taxes and that each citizen has a different demand function, that is, the amount each individual will be prepared to pay in taxes for different amounts of the good in question. Weisbrod then assumes that governments will produce to the level determined by the median voter's demand schedule — to the point at which there will be as many voters who want more of that public good as there are voters who want less. Of course, Weisbrod recognizes that this is not the way in which governments really determine the level of public expenditure, although the bargaining processes of democratic politics may come close to it. The actual way in which government sets the level of public expenditure on that service is ultimately irrelevant to the argument. So long as the assumption that different voters have different demand functions remains true, there will always be some citizen-voters who are undersatisfied with the level of production of the public good, and some citizen voters who are overtaxed by that level. The overtaxed do not have many options. They may be able to exert political pressure to lower the output-tax level, but if they fail, they can only put up with it or emigrate from the jurisdiction — obviously easier where the services are provided (and the tax raised) by a unit of local government than by a unit of national government. The undersatisfied, however, also have the option of supplementing public provision — which in the limiting case can be zero — by voluntary provision which, since we are dealing with goods that cannot be made the subject of market transactions, must be nonprofit. Thus Weisbrod concludes that private nonprofits will tend to supply the sorts of public goods for which there is not yet a demand from the majority of citizens or which a majority of citizens are prepared to pay for in taxation only in what a minority consider inadequate quantities.

Weisbrod's model leads to a number of conclusions that appear to be at least partially verified by history. By assuming that citizens' demand functions for public goods will be related to their incomes, he concludes that any particular class of public goods will tend to be supplied first by voluntary nonprofits, when only a minority of citizens have become sufficiently wealthy to articulate their demands, and subsequently, as the demand spreads through the population, by government. This certainly seems to have been the pattern of historic evolution. Governments hardly got into the business of paying for schools or hospitals much before the nineteenth century.

Another conclusion would also appear to be at least partially verified by history and international comparisons. This is that the more homogeneous the people being governed — the nearer they approach a situation in which all citizens want the same public goods to the same extent — the more likely it is that government will take over from the private voluntary sector the provision of public goods.

Weisbrod's model was pivotal in my own thinking about the Third Sector. It is this model that, for example, led me to question, as I do in a later chapter, the conventional wisdom that Third Sector institutions should be governed by bodies that are as representative as possible of the general body of citizens. If something is demanded by the general body of citizens, the government is more likely to supply it adequately because only government can get rid of free riders. On the other hand, what Third Sector institutions can do, and governments generally cannot do, is provide a service that is not demanded by the general body of citizens or provide a service above the level demanded by the general body of citizens. The function of Third Sector institutions is thus to voice and act on the demands not of the general body but of minorities whose demands differ in kind or in degree from those of the majority.

Although Weisbrod's model seems to me to permit some penetrating insights into the respective roles of government and voluntary agencies, I doubt whether conventional economic analysis provides wholly adequate tools for this purpose. In particular, I have difficulty with the idea of a demand function for the sort of public goods that are provided either by government alone, such as national defense, or jointly by government and Third Sector institutions, such as welfare services, subsidies for the arts, basic research, and so on. A demand function implies not only that different citizens will want such things to different extents, but also that they are able to trade off the extent of the want against the cost to be paid in taxation. I know that I — and I suggest the vast majority of citizens in any country — would be quite incapable of putting a figure on how much national defense is needed, let alone trading this off against the amount of tax I am prepared to pay for it. At most, I am sometimes prepared to say that I think the country should have more or less. There is some evidence, for example, that a majority of Americans before the 1980 presidential election thought more should be spent on national defense, but not even the most rash of public opinion pollsters would have been prepared to commit him- or herself to a figure that would have majority support.

Similar considerations apply to education, welfare services, health care, research, the arts, and so forth. People probably in most cases are prepared to make a judgment as to whether the current level of public expenditure in some field is too high or too low, but it will not be a very informed judgment, and it will very rarely be linked in the respondent's mind with a corresponding figure for the cost in terms of taxation as Weisbrod's model would require. Probably most of us most of the time do not get much beyond the level of conceptualization required to say whether we believe the country should spend or not spend anything in some area. The tools of economic analysis presuppose a degree of quantitative thinking that rarely occurs in the political area.

In the next chapter I will discuss how Third Sector institutions permit a country to come to grips with the problem of differing *views* of the public good as distinct from different *quantities* of a public good. For the present purpose, it is sufficient to say that Weisbrod is surely right in assuming some majoritarian or populist constraint — whatever its precise form — on government that makes it inevitable that government will leave numbers of citizens unsatisfied and thus leave room for such citizens to supplement the activities of government voluntarily through nonprofit organizations.

THE CATEGORICAL CONSTRAINT

Both the economics of the marketplace and the politics of the ballot box deal with preferences, but the type of information about preferences with which the two systems deal is different. The type of information with which the marketplace deals is illustrated by such statements as "if apples are 30 cents apiece, I will buy five; if they are 35 cents apiece, I will only buy three" — the familiar curvilinear demand function. The type of information with which the ballot box can deal is illustrated by such statements as: "All children are entitled to a basic education," "All citizens are entitled to police protection," and "The state should provide the means of subsistence for those who are too old or too infirm to work." The ballot box, unlike the marketplace, can provide only very crude information about the intensity of preferences or the quantity demanded. This is because, in general, the ballot box can deal only with simple binary choices — more or not more, less or not less, candidate A or candidate B. It does this both with goods and with bads — including, of course, the bad of the taxation needed to pay for the goods.

The ballot box does, however, provide a fairly good measure of the generality of a preference — say, the proportion of the population that will subscribe to some categorical statement about the state's responsibilities. The marketplace, conversely, does not need to know the generality of a preference. It is as easy to have a small market as a large one. This gives the market system a flexibility that the political system does not possess. We might recall, for example, that in Weisbrod's model only the median voter is satisfied with the level of public provision that Weisbrod assumes will be the equilibrium point under a majority-vote decision rule. For everybody else, the government is producing either too much or too little. This, incidentally, is a powerful argument against government taking over the production of goods that can be subject to market transactions.

So long as goods can be evaluated in individual exchange transactions, the market can adjust to the almost infinite variety of individual preferences and needs. The distinctive feature of government is something approaching the opposite characteristic. As Milton Friedman[6] pointed out: "The characteristic feature of action through political channels is that it tends to require or enforce substantial conformity." This is neither an accidental characteristic nor a human failing on the part of public officials; it is a systemic constraint that flows logically from the fundamental democratic principle that all should be equal before the law.

Immanuel Kant, in the *Critique of Practical Reason*, proposed that the test of a valid moral maxim is that it should be capable of being applied universally or, as his principle is usually translated, be a "categorical imperative." Law has to be categorical — applicable universally at least within the jurisdiction — and justice requires that public policy should come close to being categorical. A policy that applied to the citizens of Manhattan but not to citizens of Brooklyn in identical circumstances would be unfair to either the citizens of Manhattan, if it discriminated against them, or to the citizens of Brooklyn, if they were the ones against whom it discriminated. I call this characteristic of action through public sector the *categorical constraint*.

The extent to which the categorical constraint will limit the freedom of action and constrain the flexibility of the public sector will vary somewhat according to the system of government. European governments, for example, seem more attached to the equal application of public policy to all citizens than does the decentralized American system, which permits greater local variation.

The private nonprofit sector has something of the market sector's flexibility, but unlike the market sector, it can apply its flexibility to public goods. Admittedly, in doing so it is liable to suffer from the predations of the free riders. But the government sector has the corresponding and opposite drawback — it is unable to allow citizens to opt out and must therefore either perpetrate the injustice of compelling citizens to contribute to a service of which they disapprove, or, if those who disapprove of the service are sufficiently numerous and powerful, fail to produce a service needed by a deserving group. In the vast majority of cases — all those in which the citizenry is not homogeneous in the sense of having identical demands for public goods — government will be doing both — failing to produce a service needed by some citizens and compelling others to contribute to a service (or a level of service) of which they disapprove.

The government sector, in the sense in which we have defined it, cannot escape the categorical constraint. It springs from a characteristic of law, and we define government as based on an authority liable to be enforced by law. The paradox is that the categorical constraint springs from an aspect of justice — equality before the law — and seems necessarily to lead to this injustice as soon as government departs from measures for which there is unanimous consent.

At a less fundamental level, the categorical constraint is also irksome when government needs to experiment or innovate. While experimental government policies are not totally unknown, it is, in general, difficult for a unit of government to embark on a program that is not equally available throughout its jurisdiction without risking injustice. Since a heavy investment, both in money terms and in political terms, is involved in a program that is available throughout the jurisdiction, the costs of failure are great. Government may therefore be reluctant to embark on a policy until it is sure of its feasibility. Or, alternatively, a scheme may be embarked upon prematurely, before all practical problems have been worked out. Once adopted, a program is difficult to abandon.

The private nonprofit sector is free of the categorical constraint. Even if it embarks on a program that benefits a group of citizens randomly or capriciously selected, those who have not benefited cannot legitimately claim to have been treated unjustly. Individuals or institutions administering private property can say with the owner of the vineyard in the parable: "Is it not lawful for me to do what I will with mine own?"

Government can do things on a large scale, but when it makes a mistake, it makes it on a large scale too. The private sector can much more easily do things on a small scale risking a small mistake. Everyone agrees that the Third Sector has the power to experiment. Whether it actually does so is a different matter. Looking at the programs particularly of the big foundations, one is easily appalled at how conventional they seem. Every now and again a big foundation will be in the vanguard of some new movement, but far more often their programs seem merely to be slavishly following behind the intellectual fashions of the academic and administrative worlds.

This is probably to be expected when one remembers that both the staffs and the governing bodies of the big foundations are largely drawn from the academic and administrative worlds. Yet it would for all that be a mistake to be cynical about the pioneering activities of the private voluntary sector. There is hardly any public service, apart from national defense, that was not originally pioneered by private philanthropy. Education, hospitals, services for the poor, the elderly, the disabled, the protection of children, the encouragement of the arts, housing for the needy, and scientific and social research were all supported by private philanthropy long before government became involved. What government can do is to generalize an activity and apply it on a much wider scale. It takes random charitable activities and systematizes them by the categorical constraint. As an English Committee on Charitable Trusts[7] once put it, "Historically, state action is voluntary action crystalized and *made universal*" (my emphasis).

8

The Majoritarian and Other Democratic Constraints

"Hard cases make bad law" — so runs the proverb. Underlying this proverb is what I call the categorical constraint. Law must be capable of being applied universally, and this restricts what can be done by the instrumentality of law and hence also what can be done by government. Government, however, also has to depend, at least in a democracy, on public choices.

The relationship of government decision making to public choices is both subtle and complex. Weisbrod, in the model we discussed in the last chapter, assumed that government decision making would be determined by the actual or presumed vote of a majority of citizens so that government could provide a service up to but only up to the level determined by the median voter. This was explicitly a simplifying assumption that we now need to examine more carefully.

In practice, no society of any size could put every decision to the vote and on each occasion decide according to which option received more than 50 percent of the votes. Direct democracy of this kind may have existed in classical

Athens and in the New England town meetings of colonial times. Even then I suspect that the operative rule in most cases was some form of consensus rather than majority rule. Nowadays when we speak of democracy, we normally mean representative democracy. Voting systems are used to elect representatives to make decisions on behalf of the larger population whom they represent. Because representatives need the votes of the represented population if they are to be reelected, they will be influenced by the distribution of opinions in the total population. But representative assemblies are not microcosms of the electorate, producing a mirror image of the distribution of views and attitudes in the total population. The complexity of the process of representation obscures many of the problems in the idea of majority rule and enables us to speak loosely of majority rule without facing the problems inherent in the concept.

Today, with the spread of public opinion polls based on sample surveys, we can get a much clearer idea of the distribution of opinions in the population as a whole than we could have done, say, fifty years ago. Just how representative democratic government differs from the naive view of direct democracy of the Athenian kind is strikingly illustrated by Richard Crossman. In an article in which he warned his fellow members of the English Left to avoid the lure of populist referenda he wrote, "If democracy worked in an Athenian sense, this country would still exercise the death penalty, flog young criminals, forbid abortion, repatriate immigrants, punish homosexuals, ban strikes, and abolish aid to poorer countries. But all these decisions would be opposed by the majority of those who consider themselves both radicals and democrats."[1] The list is a skillful choice of policies that could be shown, on opinion survey evidence, to be supported by a majority of the voters but rejected by governments of both parties and particularly anathema to members of the radical left. Crossman continues, "We resolve the paradox by the theory of delegated democracy, according to which only a measure which runs the gauntlet of party approval and parliamentary routine really deserves to be called the people's will." Crossman's is a peculiarly British resolution of the problem that clearly owes a great deal to Burke's theory of representation, although it is dressed in more modern institutional clothes. The problem itself, however, is essentially the same as Madison's "tyrannical majority" and Jefferson's "elective despotism."

The examples Crossman gives of issues on which the majority of the electorate would be opposed to the more liberal views of the governing elite help to identify some of the problems in majority rule. If Crossman is right that the majority of people believe that homosexuals should be punished and strikes should be banned, why do democrats who believe in the sovereignty of the people in these two instances reverse the judgment of the people? The answer most usually given is that democratic freedom involves recognizing certain fundamental freedoms or human rights that are not subject to majority rule, but this does not tell us how we discover what those fundamental rights are. Crossman was probably right about public opinion in both instances at the time he was writing. Today, there is, at least in Britain, probably a majority still opposed to strikes, but public opinion about freedom for homosexuals seems to have shifted. This raises the question of the time horizon of political decisions that is also raised in a different form by the issue of economic aid to poorer countries. Running right through Crossman's list is the problem of the role of information and specialized knowledge. Should uninformed opinions have the same weight as well-informed judgments?

ARROW'S IMPOSSIBILITY THEOREM

Before turning to these questions, we need to be more precise about what we mean by the majority rule. So far we have looked at political decisions in terms of simple binary choices — to punish homosexuals or not to punish homosexuals, to execute murderers or not to execute murderers, and so on. In practice, political decisions are much too interdependent to be treated in isolation in this way. This is more obvious if we take a typical political decision such as whether to increase welfare payments or not increase welfare payments. Quite obviously that question cannot be rationally decided without considering the cost, the way the welfare scheme is organized, the effects in related fields, and so on. Political decisions are rarely if ever simple either/or questions but rather choices between a multiplicity of alternatives. Moreover, if we try to reduce them to a series of either/or alternatives, the order in which we make the choices will affect the result.

Condorcet, an eighteenth-century French mathematician, appears to have been the first to notice that there may be more than one majority choice when there are more than two alternatives from which to choose, even though each member of the group making the choice sticks to a perfectly consistent order of preferences among the alternatives.[2] A majority can prefer A to B and B to C but C to A. With such "circular preferences" the order in which the decisions are taken will affect the result. If we decide, by majority vote, between B and C before choosing between C and A, we will end up adopting A because alternative C will have been eliminated when it was defeated by alternative B. On the other hand, if we decided between C and A first, we would end up following alternative B because alternative A would have been defeated by C.[3]

Voting is essentially a device for aggregating preferences. The welfare of any individual may be assumed to be governed by his or her own preference schedule, that is to say, the way he or she ranks his or her preferences. If we could find a way of aggregating or adding together the preferences of all the individuals who make up a society, we would have a way of judging what will best serve the welfare of that society or, in other words, a single social welfare function for that society. Going beyond the particular case of the paradox of voting, Kenneth Arrow, in his celebrated theorem, demonstrated that there is no way of aggregating the full range of logically consistent preferences that a body of individuals might have that does not either depend on some criterion other than the preferences of the individuals in the group, or lead to apparently nonsensical results such as making the social ordering depend on the preferences of a single individual regardless of the preferences of others in the group or failing to recognize that a unanimous preference must also be the social preference of the whole group.[4]

Politicians and others concerned with public policy frequently assume that we can make judgments about what the public wants in the same way as we, as individuals, can say what we want. The assumption, which is encouraged by the fact that we use the singular for collective nouns, is that we can seek to maximize the collective welfare of a community (such as a nation) in essentially the same way as we can seek to maximize our own individual welfare. Obviously Arrow's proof that it is a mathematical impossibility to construct what MacKay calls "a rational aggregation device" does not mean that we can never tell whether a course of action is in the public interest or contrary to it. It does mean, however, that so long as we stick to the basic principle of allowing each individual to decide for him- or herself what is good, it may be impossible to say which of several alternatives will be the most conducive to the public good.

William Riker maintains that this will often happen and is, indeed, "the characteristic feature of politics."[6] The problem is not just a practical problem about finding out what people want (which politicians have known about for a long time). It is a fundamental problem in the very process of putting together (or aggregating) different people's judgments of the good. The conclusion to be drawn from Arrow's paradox can be expressed in a number of different ways. Riker, for example, expresses it by saying that in politics unlike economics, "There are no fundamental equilibria to predict." We might also express it by saying that there is no single social welfare function that is necessarily preferable to every other social welfare function. I prefer to say merely that the public interest is not one but many. We cannot have one single criterion of the public interest — to be determined by a single individual or a single institution acting consistently — because ultimately the public interest is inherently ambiguous as long as we derive our notion of the public good from the diversity of choices made by the members of the public themselves.

MAJORITY PREFERENCES AND FUNDAMENTAL RIGHTS

Arrow's paradox provides a rationale for pluralism based on economic analysis but, of course, pluralism as a political philosophy is much older than that. It profoundly influenced the framers of the American Constitution. Whereas, Arrow saw the problem in terms of aggregating preferences, the framers saw the problem in terms of a conflict between majority rule (which they termed the "republican principle") and the natural rights of individual citizens. Robert Dahl, in his *A Preface to Democratic Theory,* provides a means of linking these two ways of thinking and talking about the problem. We could escape from Arrow's paradox if we were prepared to make interpersonal comparisons of welfare but, as we saw in Chapter 3, there is no practical way of measuring the relative intensity of the preferences expressed by different people. Common sense alone will tell us that even if a majority were to consider that they would enjoy killing you, your preference to stay alive should weigh more heavily in the scales than their preference for killing you — even though they may outnumber you. Moreover, the right to life is but one typical example of several natural, or fundamental, rights.

James Madison, whom we may take as typical for this purpose of the thought underlying the Constitution, was concerned about the inability of majority rule to safeguard the natural rights of minorities. The problem is at least as relevant today as it was two hundred years ago. Indeed, in many ways we are probably more worried about human rights today than we would have been in the eighteenth century. This is not to say that we understand human rights any better. There are still great problems about the whole idea of natural rights and fundamental freedoms. How are such rights to be determined? By whom should they be defined? These and similar questions still remain largely unanswered, although international agreements have to some extent codified a range of natural rights that are more or less accepted as fundamental.

Dahl does not address these questions and certainly he does not pretend to answer them. Instead, he provides a framework of analysis for identifying the cases where the conflict between the theory of natural rights and the theory of majority rule will present problems for our notion of democratic freedom. He starts by reformulating the problem in terms of preferences of different intensity. He tells us, "Intensity is almost a modern psychological version of natural rights." (In passing, I cannot help commenting that I prefer Madison's language. There is something a little inadequate about describing the gas ovens of Auschwitz as conflicting with an intense preference of the Jews to avoid extermination.) Dahl's analysis will hold so long as everybody does not hold the same natural rights to be self-evident.

Using three differing intensities — strong, moderate, and slight — Dahl considers six different types of distributions. Two present serious problems for democratic government. The first is Dahl's case of "severe symmetrical disagreement." This I will redefine to correspond to a conflict between two natural rights or freedoms each held to be fundamental by different groups.[7] Dahl rightly holds that no system of government can resolve a conflict within its jurisdiction between two sets of rights and freedoms each held to be equally fundamental by different groups of citizens.[8] This conclusion seems to me equivalent to the more conventional statement that for any state to be viable presupposes a certain degree of agreement on fundamentals among all its citizens.

Voluntary organizations are ultimately as powerless to resolve the dilemma in this case as are governments. Voluntary organizations, such as the voluntary peace movement in Northern Ireland, may be better able to bridge the gulf between the warring factions than are elected representatives who have to consider their voters. But if the two positions remain irreconcilable, they cannot ultimately resolve the issues. There are also cases in which the intervention of voluntary organizations may circumvent the problem. One current issue that presents the problem of mutually contradictory rights and freedoms is the abortion controversy. A government that forces citizens to contribute through the tax system to actions that offend their fundamental values would be unjust. But the same citizens may be able to tolerate voluntary bodies — to which they do not contribute and from whose actions they can therefore disassociate themselves — paying the cost themselves. This illustration is an example of the way in which the intervention of voluntary bodies may deescalate a case of severe symmetrical disagreement (two directly conflicting views of fundamental rights) to one of severe asymmetrical disagreement (where the larger group treats the issue as of less fundamental importance than does the smaller group). On the other hand, the problem will remain incapable of solution if both factions treat the issue as one of universally applicable fundamental rights — as currently seems to be the case with the abortion issue in the United States.

Dahl's final case is that which he terms "severe asymmetrical disagreement." This corresponds to a situation in which a weak preference of the majority would override some right or freedom that a minority held to be fundamental. Here, in contrast to the case of severe symmetrical disagreement, it should theoretically be possible to devise a safeguard so long as we assume that it is possible to distinguish weak preferences from intense preferences or, in the other language, rights held to be fundamental.

Dahl maintains that the Constitution was designed especially to provide such a safeguard. After reviewing the historical evidence, he concludes, however, that the devices designed for this purpose, notably the powers of the Supreme Court and the composition of the Senate, have not proved effective. Dahl certainly does not maintain that simple majority rule is either preferable or characteristic of the American system. What then distinguishes democracies like that of the United States from dictatorship?

> If there is anything to be said for the processes that actually distinguish democracy or polyarchy from dictatorship, it is not discoverable in the clear cut distinction between government by a majority and government by a minority. The distinction comes much closer to being one between government by a minority and government by *minorities*. As compared with the political processes of a dictatorship, the characteristics of polyarchy greatly extend the number, size and diversity of the minorities whose preferences will influence the outcome of governmental decisions.[9]

This emphasis on the power of innumerable diverse minorities characterizes not only the United States but all governments that can claim to operate in a free society. Yet the problem with government by minorities is that, to an even greater extent than majority rule, it is incapable of resolving differences in complex cases involving many different conflicting interests. The minorities when organized become veto groups having power to inhibit or prevent government initiatives leading to what James MacGregor Burns called the "deadlock of democracy."[10]

This constraint on government is often loosely described as the "majoritarian constraint," but it is both more subtle and more severe. Government must constantly avoid an overactive policy in which it risks colliding with the strongly held views and interests of groups of citizens (whether they be a minority or a majority) and, at the same time, avoid deadlock and stagnation.

Of Dahl's six possible distributions, three are most likely to occur in practice. Measures for which there is a consensus, whether with strong or weak preferences, are likely to have been enacted long ago. Severe symmetrical disagreement nobody can do anything about. So we are left with the two forms of moderate disagreement and with severe asymmetrical disagreement. It is in these and particularly in the last that voluntary organizations have the most useful role.

First, and most important, they can provide the organization that minorities need to enable their views and interests to impinge on the political process. But they also have a less obvious role in carrying out a function that government is precluded from carrying out. Let us assume that a group of citizens has an intense belief that the country needs some particular form of social service, some particular form of education, or some particular art form. It is confronted by weak opposition from the majority of its fellow citizens. In these circumstances, the government is unlikely to act. However, there is nothing to stop voluntary organizations from acting on their own — particularly, if opposition springs from reluctance to pay the cost in the form of taxation rather than opposition to the service itself.

WHEN VIEWS OF THE PUBLIC GOOD DIFFER

In this case, the conclusions we can draw from Weisbrod's economic model are remarkably similar to those we draw from Dahl's polyarchic or pluralistic political theory. The difference is that Weisbrod's model assumes agreement about the nature of the public good and that the disagreement is quantitative — how much of it people are prepared to pay for in taxation. Dahl's analysis enables us to accommodate differences as to what constitutes a public good. In the nineteenth century, for example, there would have been many, perhaps a majority, who regarded welfare payments as bad, undermining the system of *laissez faire* and the work ethic of self-sufficiency. Yet many charities date from this period, so we can assume that the more charitable minority who sacrificed their own resources to act on their belief held that belief more intensely than the opposite view held by the majority. It is this ability to tolerate different views of the public good that the pluralistic philosophy sees as the characteristic of a free society. Voluntary organizations are one of the means — indeed a necessary and essential means — of putting that philosophy into practice.

The minority with an intense preference provides what they consider to be, in the language used earlier, a public good. I argued earlier that there is an element of subjective judgment about what is to be considered a public good. The theory of polyarchy suggests that there should not be one but many views as to what is a public good. Perhaps the most important function of a voluntary Third Sector is to broaden the range, and the diversity within the range, of public goods. In a free society there should be room for many views as to what the country needs. Voluntary organization enables these views to be expressed and the goods provided without commiting others to that view or compelling them to contribute to their cost.

Should there be no constraint, therefore, on the ability of organized minorities voluntarily to provide whatever they feel would be a public good? The theory suggests at least two constraints. First, their view of a public good should not collide with an equally intense view that it is a public bad. A hypothetical example would be an organization that believed in distributing free drugs to teenagers. In this particular case the constraint obviously would take the form of prohibition by law. The second constraint arises from placing the case in the context of severe or moderate asymmetrical disagreement but extends somewhat beyond this, qualifying what we mean by the weak opposition of the majority. For society to recognize the purpose as charitable, not only must the providers of the good believe that it is good for society, but society must be satisfied in some way — for example, by some judicial process — that the view that it is good is a reasonable one to hold, whether or not a majority of the citizens hold it. An example would be a religion or ethical system to which a majority of citizens do not subscribe.[11] Less emotive examples would be minority educational theories, minority health theories, minority interests in the arts, and controversial forms of social service.

PUBLIC SUBSIDY AND TAX EXEMPTION

This argument suggests that a "free" society, to be worthy of the adjective, must at least recognize the right to exist of any organization meeting these requirements. Whether it should also receive special privileges such as tax exemption is really a separate question. In the Anglo-American world, charities have been exempt from direct taxation for so long that the two questions have become almost inextricably confused. Yet providing a public benefit without the incentive of private gain need not necessarily imply tax exemption. There is clearly a strong *prima facie* case for the state encouraging such activity, but whether to do so by tax exemption or otherwise depends not only on how far but also on how the state decides to encourage any particular activity. In France, for example, there is no general principle that charitable activities are tax exempt, but a large range of charitable activities benefit from a variety of tax privileges and tax subsidies.

A modern state can make a finely graduated response, and we can identify at least five steps along a scale running from positive discouragement and prohibition to total subsidy:

(1) Starting at the negative end, the organization may actually be penalized. This is rare in the Anglo-American world (except for seditious or treasonable organizations) but nineteenth-century France would provide examples in the form of the penalties imposed on religious orders and private education.

(2) The organization is subject to tax much like a for-profit organization — except, of course, that it will not normally have profits to tax. Otherwise it is not subject to any further disabilities. Typical examples would be political parties and other organizations with primarily political objectives. Obviously, political participation is something a democratic state should encourage. Use of the instrument of tax exemption, however, would unduly facilitate the conversion of wealth into political influence. The modern solution has tended to be to use forms of direct subsidy, for example, an element of public subsidy for the political campaigns of candidates for public office. (But this solution is not wholly satisfactory.)

(3) The organization itself is tax exempt but donors get no tax advantages from contributing to it. In the United States this is the position of organizations not covered by Section 501 (c)(3) but by other paragraphs of Section 501.

(4) The organization is tax exempt itself and the donors may also deduct their contributions to it from their income assessable to tax.

(5) The organization, over and above its tax privileges, also receives direct subsidies from compulsorily raised public revenues. The subsidies may be linked to tax-deductible contributions — as in the case of matching grants — thus accentuating the effects of tax deductability, or the subsidies may be based on some other criterion. Subsidies may represent a large or small part of the organization's resources.

(6) In the other extreme case, the organization may be wholly dependent on public subsidy.

While subsidies and tax privileges are both methods of encouraging the flow of resources in the direction desired by the state, there is an important difference in principle between the two that is sometimes forgotten. Naive economists, in particular, are liable to argue that since tax exemption reduces the amount of tax that would otherwise be raised, the cost of the exemption should be treated as the equivalent of a subsidy. Yet a subsidy is paid out of money that has entered the public purse and for which the public authorities are, in consequence, answerable to the electorate. Money contributed to a private organization, even if relieved of the burden of taxation, has never entered the public purse. Public subsidies are thus subject to the constraints on government we have already discussed, whereas private contributions are not. The use of tax exemption and tax deductibility enables government to adopt the interesting intermediate position of encouraging some activity without actually accepting responsibility for it,[12] for example, would-be contributions to charities. In effect, the government is able to say to the contributors, "We recognize that what you are doing can be seen as a public benefit and you see it in this light yourselves, but the public benefit is not sufficiently widely desired or recognized for us to be entitled to compel all taxpayers to contribute to it."

My argument throughout this chapter has been that government and politics are inherently constrained — subject, if you will, to government failure much as the commercial system is subject to market failure — and a free society needs to be able on occasion to "depoliticize" just as much as to "demarketize" services. The charitable sector is a way of providing a "depoliticized" public service. I suspect that a curious feature of the English law of charities reflects this instinctive suspicion of the political process although probably unconsciously. Unlike most questions of public policy in Britain, the definition of charity and hence tax exemption have remained a matter for the courts (rather than for either government or Parliament) to determine, so that the definition of charity has never been politicized.

The extreme case of the private organization wholly dependent on public subsidy obviously cannot be justified on these grounds. Yet governments quite often use and, sometimes specially establish, technically private organizations to carry out some function that is entirely financed by the public purse. The reasons for this seem to have less to do with the constraints discussed so far (which derive from the nature of law and the problems of aggregating preferences) and more with accidental characteristics of government, which I call the "minor constraints."

THE TIME HORIZON CONSTRAINT

In several of the examples given by Crossman (in the passage quoted above), the difference between representative government and simple majority rule fits comfortably into the natural rights argument analyzed by Dahl — the punishment of homosexuals, the repatriation of immigrants, the banning of strikes. One of his instances, however, is aid to poorer countries, and this is better analyzed on a different criterion: the distinction between a decision made on a short and one made on a long time horizon. On a short time horizon calculation, it is unlikely that most people would wish to reduce their current incomes through taxation to aid poorer countries. Yet quite apart from any altruistic motive, a strong case can be made that it is in the long-term interests of the advanced countries to provide developmental aid to the underdeveloped countries. For most people, the act of casting a vote — or, for that matter, answering an opinion pollster's questionnaire — is not likely to warrant much careful calculation and thus likely to reflect a short-term view of their interests. Crossman's argument is, of course, that representatives charged with responsibility of using their own judgment in the interests of their constituents may be expected to take a rather longer view of the country's interests than their constituents will spontaneously do themselves. We need to note, however, that as Samuel Brittan has argued,[13] the terms of the competitive struggle for the people's vote often tends, in practice, to make politicians themselves into short-term maximizers.

We can generalize and postulate a fairly simple relationship between the time horizon of decision and the accountability to which the decision makers are subject. At one extreme, in the political field, the shortest time horizon would be encouraged by a system in which the politicians would immediately be accountable to the spontaneously expressed views of their voters — government by public opinion poll. From this we could move to real governments, like those of present-day Britain or the United States, faced by relatively volatile electorates and, then, to governments like that of France under DeGaulle that are more secure and capable of taking a longer term view of the country's interest. At the other end of the scale we find the benevolent despot, who is free to exercise his or her judgment of the country's best interests on a long time horizon — although he or she is, of course, only too prone to misjudge them. Leaving aside the danger of misjudgment, the more immediate the accountability, the stronger the feedback and the shorter the time horizon against which decisions will be made.

This scale can be replicated both in the market sector and in the private philanthropic Third Sector. In much the same way as governments may be more or less immediately responsive to the demands of their electorates, so too in the market context we find, depending on the degree of competition, firms more or less immediately responsive to the market. We will find opportunist businesses exploiting any market opening that may arise but having little scope to make judgments on a long time horizon, and large business corporations that have clearly developed plans for the future extending over decades responding sluggishly to market demands when these contradict their long-term plans. If I understand him correctly, it is on this ability to make decisions on a longer time horizon that Schumpeter[14] relied in his contention that big businesses have had more to do with raising living standards than with keeping them down and in his defense of oligopolistic practices.

In the Third Sector, the same scale applies also. Organizations depending on day-to-day contributions are constrained to concentrate on those activities that make an immediate appeal to their contributors. At the far end of the scale would be the great institutional foundations, like Carnegie, Rockefeller, and Ford, which are only weakly accountable to any constituency. Simon Kuznets makes the interesting observation that institutions can and often do make decisions on a longer time horizon than do individuals, behaving at times almost as if "they were endowed with eternal life."[15] This is how we would expect the great foundations to behave, supplementing the activities of government with investments beyond the time horizon to which governments are constrained and possibly also beyond the time horizons of the market sector. In fact, we do find foundations acting in this way. The classic example would be the "green revolution" pioneered by the Rockefeller Foundation and subsequently financed by a number of other foundations (including the Ford Foundation) and by intergovernmental agencies, which similarly are less immediately accountable to any constituency.

The green revolution is today occasionally criticized on grounds that imply doubts about the time horizon. The critics maintain that the development of higher-yielding cereals and other foodstuffs pays insufficient attention to the long-term effects of such an agricultural revolution on the ecological balance of the planet and the social structure of the countries in which it takes place. This merely emphasizes that even when we are dealing with something as fundamental and long term as how the human race will feed itself — throughout the world and for generations to come — there is no one correct solution. Here, too, there is a need for a plurality of approaches and a need for redundancy in case the chosen solution fails. The voluntary sector provides a means of articulating such alternatives and, to a limited extent, acting upon them. The great philanthropic institutions acting on very long-term problems, like the other philanthropic organizations acting on more short-term problems, can provide this distinctive contribution of the Third Sector: pluralism and redundancy.

Time horizon calculations are closely related to the problem of indeterminate risk. In general, the more long term an investment, the greater the risk attached to it. When the risk is calculable, the commercial sector will usually be able to deal with it. The expected yield from such an investment needs to be sufficient to offset the costs of deferred consumption and cover the risk of failure. Where, however, the risks are indeterminate and incalculable, the commercial sector will find it difficult to act, and the nonprofit sector will have greater opportunity to carry out its historic role of pioneering and experimentation — as long as the institutions are not made to be accountable too soon. In these circumstances, the absence of strong measures of accountability, far from being a weakness of the Third Sector, becomes a strength enabling it to undertake experiments, the benefits of which are too uncertain and too long term to be undertaken by either the commercial or the governmental sector.

THE KNOWLEDGE CONSTRAINT

Whether decisions are made on a long or a short time horizon, they require knowledge. Contrary to the view of the cynics, governments usually place a great deal of weight on informed opinion. Indeed, one would probably get a better approximation to the way decisions are actually made in democratic governments if one assumed the decisions in any given field of policy followed the balance of expert opinion than if one assumed that they followed the balance of voters' opinions. Governments frequently develop their own experts. The Northcote-Trevelyan reforms, which led to the establishment of the British civil service, were a conscious effort to establish a class of professional administrators whose expertise was originally conceived as generally applicable throughout the field of public administration. France, with the establishment of the *Grandes Ecoles* in Napoleonic times and, more recently, the *Ecole Nationale d'Administration,* has also set up its own firms in the knowledge industry. The United States is characterized by an exceptionally open system of demand for policy-relevant knowledge, freely drawing into the public sector experts from universities, business, and the private sector generally, and contracting out to private sector institutions like the Rand Corporation, for knowledge in specialized fields.

Knowledge is, however, never adequate for policy. Relatively monolithic systems of government, like that of the United Kingdom, tend to develop orthodoxies that may obscure alternative approaches to the problems facing government. The United States, with competition between the institutions of the executive and the legislative branches and competition between agencies within the executive branch, can generate a greater range of options. Even so, the task of monitoring and criticizing can more effectively be carried out by institutions outside the public sector. Perhaps even more important is that public officials will almost inevitably tend to think in terms of action by government running the risk of insufficient weight being given to the possibilities of non-governmental solutions.[16]

The public need for policy-relevant knowledge provides scope for a whole range of specialized institutions in the Third Sector — university departments concerned with policy-relevant disciplines, schools of public policy, research institutions, and bodies like the Brookings Institution or the American Enterprise Institute.[17]

For convenience, I am including the knowledge constraint among the other constraints on government. In fact, however, it is a constraint of a somewhat different kind. It is not a case of government at a relative disadvantage compared to the voluntary sector. There is no particular impediment to government adding to its stock of policy-relevant knowledge. It is rather a case in which government can never, in practice, generate as much knowledge as it needs but in which, nonetheless, the independent voluntary sector can perform its traditional role of contributing an element of diversity and redundancy.

Another problem flows from the categorical constraint. Not only should all be treated equally; all must be seen to be treated equally. In practical terms, this means that administrators applying public policy must follow rules — rules that ensure that two identical cases are treated the same by different administrators and rules that are publicly defensible. Since there is a vast range of circumstances for which provision must be made, we get the typical morass of bureaucratic red tape with questionable and often ridiculous borderline cases. To take an example from the field of welfare payments, clearly the wife of a man with a normal income should not be entitled to welfare payments even though she may have no income of her own. Yet at what stage of cohabitation does a man take over from the state the responsibility for the financial maintenance of the woman with whom he is living? The welfare authorities in both England and the United States have had to wrestle with this naughty problem and have made themselves somewhat ridiculous in the process. More important, the rules ultimately become a barrier between the objectives of the policy and their implementation. This is particularly the case with welfare schemes, the clients of which are often ill-educated and frightened by the bureaucratic requirements.

In the times of adversity and crisis in which welfare schemes are designed to help, the first line of defense in most cases is not the state services or the services of voluntary organizations but rather the spontaneous and informal help and support that family, friends and neighbors give to each other. The Wolfenden Committee[18] described this as "the informal system of social helping." Although impossible to quantify, the volume of resources transferred within this system in terms of voluntary labor, psychological support, and a significant volume of material resources is certainly very considerable indeed. It may even begin to approach the volume of resources transferred within the quantified and monetarized market sector. It is also, of course, almost certainly free of bureaucratic constraints. Nonetheless, what the informal system can provide is severely limited. It cannot normally provide professional expertise, expensive plant, or prolonged financial support. A mother or an aunt may nurse a child through a bout of flu but cannot take out the child's inflamed appendix. Friends and neighbors may provide a temporary home for a recently bereaved widower but, save in the wealthiest circles, cannot maintain him during a prolonged period of unemployment or incapacity. An older sister or a classmate may give a young bride some useful advice on how to cope with her mother-in-law but is unlikely to be of much help when it comes to suing the landlord.

The contention of the Wolfenden Committee was that for the purpose of strengthening the informal system of social helping and providing the benefits of minimal organization, voluntary organizations are particularly well adapted and far better adapted than is a government agency constrained by bureaucratic rules. A group of tenants meeting informally can develop into a Tenants Association, parents and teachers meeting informally can crystalize into a properly established Parent Teachers Association, and so on. What I have called the "time horizon constraint" and the "knowledge constraint" both point to a role for Third Sector organizations that is relatively formally structured. This "bureaucratic constraint" on government agencies, on the other hand, points to a role for Third Sector bodies that may not even qualify as "organizations." Such "self-help" groups are, in many respects, close to the pattern of mutual benefit associations (such as the professional body, the trade union, the club, and the friendly society) but may lack their degree of formal organization. In the words of the Wolfenden report, "In the space between the loosely structured informal system and the more strictly organized statutory system, people can use the medium of the voluntary organization to join with others in devising means to meet their own needs or those of others they wish to help."

Seymour Sarason and his colleagues[19] have demonstrated how informal networks of resource exchange can flourish and mobilize resources that are not mobilized by the formal organizations of commerce and government. This is precisely because they are not formally organized and have not acquired a professional ethos. In his view, the professional ethos delimits and tends to define the personality in terms of specialized roles and prevents people redefining themselves as resources for themselves and for others.

Yet the informal system is in need of reinforcement. There are quantitative and qualitative limits to what it can do. Moreover, the informal system is constantly being weakened by demographic and social changes. This is not necessarily because the informal system has been superseded or supplanted by statutory services. It is not the development of statutory social services but social and geographic mobility that have destroyed the three-generation family household. Nor is the disappearance of the three-generation family household the only factor weakening the informal system. So far as the informal system is concerned, the increasing proportion of married women going out to work, the tendency to substitute for communal leisure activities either paid entertainment (like the theater or spectator sports) or private entertainment (like television) and the decline of churchgoing are all having the same effect.

9

Summary and Some Conclusions

This book is a critique of an argument. The argument seeks to explain why democratic, capitalist societies characteristically include a sector in which resources are allocated neither by the typically capitalist mechanisms of market economics nor by the authority of democratically elected governments. The argument is not historical. It seeks to show *why* a Third Sector is logically required by the limitations of both market economics and democratic politics rather than *how,* historically, the Third Sector arose. There may be a few nonprofit institutions that have wrested a role away from government or commercial institutions, but what has happened far more often is that a role previously undertaken by private nonprofit institutions has been taken over by government or commercial institutions.

The argument does, however, cast some light on why certain roles have moved into the sphere of government or commerce while others have tended to remain in the Third Sector, which the argument sees as a residual. Thus, for example, the "free rider problem" casts a good deal of light on the forces that have tended to shift roles into the government sector. The "primeval soup" of the political economy was probably something like the "informal system" of social helping within the family and between neighbors that, in its contemporary form, is described by the Wolfenden Committee. The primitive political economy was relatively undifferentiated, and it is only quite late in the history of Western civilization that the respective roles of family, government, commerce, and philanthropy can be at all clearly differentiated. Even today the boundaries between the responsibilities of each sector are not immutably drawn and are a constant source of political controversy.

We should therefore be rightly wary of the argument if it pretended to offer rigid definitions of what ought to be the responsibilities of government or the responsibilities of commerce and what should be left to voluntary action through the Third Sector. The argument, however, does not pretend to do this. Instead, it identifies the conditions under which institutions in each sector are likely to perform best and thus provides a framework for judging in which sector an activity is likely to be most effectively undertaken given the actual conditions. Thus the easier it is to organize an activity on the basis of *quid pro quo* exchange transactions, the more effectively will institutions of the commercial sector operate; the more an activity (that cannot be organized on the basis of exchange transactions) is considered to be universally required by all citizens, the more appropriate it will be to entrust it to institutions of government.

The argument itself is a two-step argument with an economic aspect and a political aspect. It so happens that the economic aspect has been developed in far greater detail than the political aspect, but the two are intimately related.

Oscar Wilde defined a cynic as a man who knows the price of everything and the value of nothing. This distinction between value and price lies quite close to the idea of externalities to which I referred in summarizing the economic theory of market failure. When we say that education or art is a "public good" or "carries positive externalities," what we mean is that their value is greater than any price we may have paid for them. When we place a value on society that succors the poor, the weak, and the infirm, it is a value that cannot be evaluated in any marketplace. Going somewhat beyond Wilde's aphorism, we can speak of the richness of society using "richness" in a sense that cannot be measured by the gross national product or by any conventional economic measure. But whereas price has a generally accepted meaning that can be expressed in common units of measurement, this meaning of richness will vary from individual to individual. To one, it may mean a society that places a value beyond price on the excellence of its artistic or cultural achievements. To another, it may mean a society that places a value beyond price on social justice or on freedom. To a third, it may mean a society that places a value beyond price on respect for the natural environment. In each of these cases — and in the many other examples that could be given — citizens perceive values that are not fully reflected by the economic system.

The characteristic of democratic or, as Robert Dahl would call it, polyarchal society is that it tolerates a greater variety and diversity in the ranking of these values. An authoritarian or theocratic society can impose a single ranking of values because this ranking is seen either as given by God or determined and deduced from a single theory of what is good for society — whereas the characteristic of what in the West we call a free society is that the ranking of values is seen as determined by the free choice of the members of that society themselves. The capitalist market system makes a very good job of this responsiveness to individual choice where the values are personal and self-regarding. When an individual places a value greater than its price on some article that he or she wants for him- or herself, he or she can buy it. Buyer and seller will then both be better off, and the market will have performed its magic of aggregating preferences precisely as Pareto described.

The problem arises when the values are not personal but social: where the individual wants something not for him- or herself but for society. Where such social values are widely held in common, governments can act. Complete unanimity is, of course, rare and not usually required, and the extent of support for the dominant value is, in practice, less important than are the extent and intensity of opposition. Where the social values conflict in fundamental and basic ways, the problem becomes insoluble and ultimately the society disintegrates into violence and civil war. But where social values diverge in ways that are, rather literally, tolerable, a voluntary Third Sector permits different and inconsistent social values to be pursued concurrently. Quite often, of course, the divergence will not be about the direction of social policy so much as differences on questions of degree. In most Western democracies, there is likely to be a fair degree of consensus about the need for some form of welfare program, some form of support for the arts, some degree of environmental protection, and so on. Controversies on these topics much more often take the form of arguments between those who think that too much is being required and those who think that too little is required. A voluntary Third Sector will in these cases enable those who want more to give more without forcing others to do the same.

This is the essential reason for that part of the Third Sector that is concerned with social objectives. It it not merely physically but logically impossible for government to pursue the full range and diversity of social goals that its citizens seek. The range of diverse goals that the society as a whole can pursue is increased by voluntary social action that supplements the social action government can demand of all citizens and will be increased still further by tolerating social action for which government need take no responsibility itself.

In the Third Sector broadly interpreted to include all private nonprofit organizations, we also find organizations—such as mutual associations, trade unions, professional associations, and clubs — that are not necessarily concerned with objectives of social value.[1] In these organizations, the benefits may be quite as internalized as in a commercial undertaking. There is no particular difficulty in explaining why government will normally be inappropriate to take on the roles they perform in society, since they are established to provide benefits for themselves rather than for the generality of citizens and thus would normally fall foul of both the categorical and the majoritarian constraints.

We still need, however, to explain why their members choose — and in some cases have no other option but to choose — the nonprofit form rather than the for-profit commercial form of the business sector. Because the benefits may be internal to the organization, the language of externalities does not readily provide an explanation, but the much more flexible language of transaction costs can probably do so.[2] Characteristically, the benefits members derive from these forms of nonprofit organizations are so difficult to pin down that it would be difficult, and in some cases impossible, to make them the subject of *quid pro quo* transactions. The nonprofit form, in effect, enables members to say "without specifying exactly what benefits we seek from this organization, such benefits as arise shall be divided up among us."

In summary, therefore, the argument with which this book has been concerned enables us to derive from the ideas of pluralism and constraints on government, roles and functions that will be better carried out by private endeavor than by government and to derive, from the concepts of market failure and transaction costs, roles and functions that would be more or less difficult — and in the limting case impossible — to formulate as marketable transactions. Thus it helps to explain the existence of a Third Sector subject neither to the discipline of the marketplace nor to that of the ballot box. But what practical lessons can we derive from this theoretical argument? In conclusion, I would like to suggest three or four such practical lessons.

Perhaps the most obviously topical today is the role of Third Sector institutions as a supplement to the agencies and services of government. In the United States and throughout Western Europe we have seen a phenomenon that journalists call "taxpayer revolt." It may take somewhat different forms. In the United States and in Britain, for example, its main manifestation seems to have been an orderly and constitutional shift to the political right, whereas in Italy, it seems to have taken the form of black markets and moonlighting as producers and consumers, employers and employees conspire to avoid taxes and social security contributions by carrying out their transactions outside the legitimate marketplace.

In politics events rarely have a single cause, and electorates, as far as we can judge from opinion surveys, display almost an infinite capacity for concurrently maintaining mutually contradictory or inconsistent opinions. Nonetheless there does seem to have been a significant shift in the balance between the level of social expenditure the majority of the electorate demands and the amount of taxation it is prepared to pay to maintain it. This fits very neatly into the economic model devised by Burton Weisbrod discussed in Chapter 7. We would need to assume, which is not improbable, that the "output-tax level" of Weisbrod's model — that is to say, the point of balance between the level of taxation and the level of welfare expenditure — had been determined in response to well-articulated and fairly intense preferences of a minority but is now above the level that would be chosen by a majority of citizens. As we have seen, it is far from certain that many people actually succeed in relating the level of welfare services they consider desirable to the level of taxes for which they are prepared to pay. Weisbrod's "output-tax level" is thus, something we have to deduce rather than pick up directly from opinion polls. However, insofar as a shift in the political balance has taken place in recent years, we might be able to explain it simply in organizational terms — the fairly recent development of organizations to express and articulate the weaker preferences of the opposed majority. But the more probable explanation is, I think, somewhat different.

In its early stages, the costs of welfare in terms of taxation were not unduly burdensome for the majority of the citizens. A progressive tax system ensures that the burden of taxation is borne disproportionately by the wealthier minority. It is only when the costs of welfare grow to the point at which they amount to a significant proportion of the national income that they require a broadening of the tax base. Moreover, the development of the welfare state coincided with a period of exceptionally fast economic growth. It is much easier to forego income one never had than to suffer an actual cut in one's standard of living. It is only quite recently that the combined effects of the expansion of social service expenditure and the slowing down of economic growth have meant that the majority have had to face a cut in their posttax real income.

Even in such circumstances, Weisbrod's model suggests that there will be a minority that believe in a higher level of social services than that for which most of their fellow citizens are prepared to pay. The model also suggests the solution. That minority will have to bear voluntarily the additional cost themselves. In some ways this may be no bad thing. Milton Friedman's gibe was shrewd when he wrote that "the fundamental fallacy of the welfare state is the attempt to do good at somebody else's expense." It is too easy to adopt a posture of liberality if one knows that one can share the cost of that liberality with 50,000,000 other people who may not wish to share that posture. Richard Titmuss was almost certainly wrong in his mystical belief that a government generous with the taxpayers' money would somehow mold its citizens' attitudes toward a spirit of generosity. It is much more likely that the example of the few who voluntarily make sacrifices for the good of others will spread the ideals of care and generosity and ultimately work through to the attitudes of the majority.

Apart from the reluctance of taxpayers to pay its cost, there is another factor that limits the extent to which the government sector can take over the role of social care. This is what I have called the bureaucratic constraint. The government can command resources in one of two ways. The first is direct compulsion. Thus, for example, parents can be compelled to provide for their children or compulsory military service can require citizens to devote part of their lives to the defense of their country. The second is a more indirect form: The state raises money by compulsory taxation and uses the money to purchase specialized labor to perform the service.

For many of the services provided by the government sector — defense, the maintenance of law and order, the administration of justice, education, even many kinds of health care — a specialized professional service constrained by bureaucratic rules need present no major problem. At the very least, its benefits are likely to outweigh its disadvantages. But as the welfare state begins to deal with less easily defined social problems — such as those of family relations, child care, care of old people, moral support for those suffering from some social and physical disabilities — the balance of advantage between the specialized professional and a voluntary service will be altered. In some of these cases no great skill, but only a willingness to devote time and sympathy, is required. In others, there may be no agreed body of technique to be transmitted by professional education so that the client requires a choice of alternative services that a state service will always find difficulty in providing. In nearly all these cases bureaucratic rules will be exceptionally hampering, since the person providing the service needs to make a personal commitment to the client undistracted by loyalty to his or her professional colleagues or considerations of administrative efficiency and equity. In many of these types of cases, the service will be best provided by volunteers who are themselves fellow sufferers from the same disability as the client and thus in a position instinctively to understand and sympathize with the client's problem.

There are, of course, satisfactions in voluntary service of this kind. Like the quality of mercy, voluntary service blesses him or her that gives and him or her that takes. The large organizations of both government and the commercial sector are often remote and frequently give the individual little feeling of participation in the good being done, even when the individual, as a taxpayer, is paying for it. There is a satisfaction and a sense of fulfillment that these other sectors all too rarely provide to be derived from doing something oneself about a social problem. For the volunteer, to some extent, the work is its own reward — the process is the output. Voluntary organizations can provide the institutional framework for this.

This is a theme that has been developed by Peter Berger and Richard Neuhas in *To Empower the People*. They suggest that we are witnessing in the United States (and, although they are less concerned with this, in Western Europe also) a historically unprecedented dichotomy between public and private life. Meaning, fulfillment, and personal identity are realized in the private sphere, while the large institutions of the state and of capitalist enterprise, which they call the "megastructures," are typically alienating. The individual is constantly having to migrate between the megastructures and private life. When the welfare state operates through the megastructures, this tendency is accentuated. There are, however, institutions standing between the individual in his or her private life and the large institutions of public life. These they term "mediating structures." They argue that mediating structures are essential for a vital democratic society, and they recommend that public policy should protect and foster mediating structures and, wherever possible, utilize them for the realization of social purposes. For Berger and Neuhaus mediating structures are not entirely synonymous with nonprofit organizations, but the smaller — as they would say, "human-sized" — voluntary organizations definitely come within their definition of mediating structures. In this conception of the role of voluntary organizations as mediating structures they are more than merely supplements to the activities of the public sector; they are, like the public sector itself, part of the means by which, in conjunction and in harmony with the public sector, society expresses and acts out its social purposes.

For all these reasons, we can expect that, in the last quarter of the twentieth century, the structure of the welfare state will subtly change. The component of public finance and professional service will diminish, at least relatively, and the component of private funding and volunteer services will need to increase and the two become more closely allied. These changes have already begun to take place. There are merits in this but also problems.

The boundaries between public and private philanthropy will tend to become obscured. Public subsidy of private voluntary organizations is used when the public authorities want to take advantage of the greater flexibility and humanity of voluntary service. At the same time, something like private subsidy of public services occurs when social workers draw on private funds to meet needs that cannot be met from public funds or when volunteers join with the professionals of the public service. This obscuring of the boundary between public and the private sectors makes the problem of accountability more difficult. When the boundaries are clear cut, the problem of accountability is, at least conceptually, also relatively clear-cut. The public services are accountable to the public authorities. The private institutions are accountable to their members or to donors, and public supervision need be no more obtrusive than Carlyle's "constable in the marketplace." However, when an institution is effectually dependent on an inextricable mix of public and private resources, the public and private elements will each seek to use their respective contributions to gain control. The market failure/government constraints rationale gives us few clues as to how this particular problem can be resolved. Yet particularly in social services, such mixed institutions are already numerous and in all probability are going to grow in importance.

The resources of the Third Sector are limited. Admittedly, they may be less limited than is often supposed. It could well be that improvements in fund raising and more imaginative methods of enlisting volunteers than those currently used could considerably increase the Third Sector's resources. Nonetheless, it remains a truism that insofar as the resources of the Third Sector are used to supplement government services or take over services abandoned by government, those resources are not available for performing the distinctive services that cannot be provided by government. The principal distinctive contributions of the Third Sector institutions are a greater diversity than government can provide and greater scope than government possesses for experimentation. When governments pull out of the provision of social services in the expectation that these will be taken over by voluntary charities, an indirect cost will be a loss of diversity within the system as a whole and less scope for the Third Sector to indulge in its traditional role of experimentation and pioneering. As we have already seen, there are certain advantages in shifting responsibility for social services from the government to the Third Sector. The danger, however, is that if Third Sector institutions are too compliant in taking over services from government in a period when public expenditure is being restricted, their resources will become disproportionately committed to maintaining services for which there is a general demand to the detriment of their role in providing services for which there is only a minority demand. They may find it more difficult in future to look further ahead of the popular will than governments can afford to do. Yet this was one of their distinctive contributions. Given that neither governmental nor Third Sector institutions can know in advance exactly what the majority of voters will demand, the rational strategy for a Third Sector, in a period of government retrenchment, is to avoid too readily taking over from government services that they believe to be popular. If public clamor develops, the government may be forced to reinstate the program. In the meantime Third Sector institutions can continue to concentrate on those programs that appeal to their own idiosyncratic constituencies.

This may sound like an unduly cynical strategy, but it corresponds to the relative strengths and weaknesses of the government and the Third Sector. Governments are never perfectly representative. Indeed, as we saw in Chapter 8, there are inherent contradictions in the concept of perfect representation. Nonetheless, it is mere arrogance to suppose that we can devise better representative systems to control philanthropy than we have been able to devise for government. If we are looking for organizations that will provide what most citizens believe to be required, then we should either look to the existing institutions of government or reform those institutions. The distinctive role of the Third Sector is, on the contrary, to provide the organizational framework that will enable minorities — including minorities who consider themselves better informed or wiser than the majority — to provide what they believe to be required as distinct from those things that would be generally accepted as necessary.

There must, of course, be constraints on Third Sector institutions. Like all organizations, they must keep within the law and not indulge in activities that will infringe on the fundamental rights of others. But within these broad constraints, they will serve their distinctive purpose best by serving sectional interests and advancing sectional views rather than seeking to duplicate the representative function of government.

Certain consequences flow from this view of Third Sector institutions as nonmajoritarian and certain problems too. It has been fashionable for some years now to argue that the controlling bodies of Third Sector institutions — particularly the trustees of private foundations and the boards of public charities — should become more representative, that their composition should reflect more closely the social and demographic composition of the population at large. The emphasis here seems to me misplaced and to be confusing the distinctive role of the Third Sector as a source of diversity in society with the representative role of government as a channel for the expression of the popular will.

Admittedly, an institution that has grown stale may be reinvigorated by introducing into its governing bodies persons with different backgrounds when the intellectual capital of the original founders seems to have become exhausted. Thus women on a previously all male board, blue-collar workers on a previously middle-class board, or blacks on a previously all-white board may serve to bring in new ideas and new approaches. But this is very different from a general policy of ensuring that the boards of private foundations regularly include the appropriate quota of women, blue-collar workers, and blacks. The danger in the latter policy is that the search for balance will weaken commitment and dedication to the distinctive cause of the institution. When Third Sector institutions represent and have to reconcile diverging interests, they run the risk of blurring their own sense of vocation.

In an ideal world, all sectional interests and all sectional views would have an equal chance of establishing institutions to represent those interests and views. In the real world this is not the case. Some sectional interests can command greater resources either of money or of organizing ability (or both) to support their views than can other sectional interests. The desire to correct this imbalance is presumably the reason for the efforts to achieve more balanced representation in the governing bodies of voluntary organizations. Yet the logic of the situation should lead not to the attempt to make existing voluntary organizations cover a wider range but rather to encourage the establishment of new organizations that will represent the underrepresented sections of society.

At the same time there are dangers in too single-minded a dedication to narrowly defined objectives. These dangers would exist even if the ideal were achieved and the Third Sector comprised such a comprehensive range of voluntary organizations that every sectional interest were represented. All democratic governments rely heavily on voluntary organizations to represent sectional interests and views. The sort of representative democracy we know would be impossible without voluntary organizations. They range from the political parties themselves through a wide diversity of pressure groups, interest groups, and lobbies to charitable bodies — whose charters may prohibit them from any direct impact on the political system but whose activities nonetheless serve to bring their particular concerns into the public eye.

Voluntary organizations serve to voice and articulate the views of minorities and thus ensure that the full diversity of views of a free society gets represented. But the task of reconciling those views and of formulating the rules by which conflicting views and interests are to be weighed and balanced belongs to the political system itself. As we saw in Chapter 8 when considering Robert Dahl's analysis of the Madisonian problem of majority tyranny, no political system can resolve the situation that Dahl describes as "severe symmetrical disagreement," that is to say, where there is a conflict between two sets of intense preferences or two views of society each held to be fundamental by different groups within that society. Where the conflict is particularly intense, where the conflicting views are on matters for which citizens are prepared to die and to kill, the society will ultimately disintegrate into violence and civil war. Where the conflict is somewhat less intense, the result is simply deadlock. Voluntary organizations do serve to express the diversity of views in the free society and thus enable the political system to take them into account. In the ideal situation voluntary organizations may enable intense preferences of the minority to be voiced and avoid a majority with weak preferences from overriding rights held to be fundamental by that minority. However, in practice, voluntary organizations also frequently serve to intensify preferences and thus increase the possibility of deadlock — although fortunately only in very rare cases do they escalate emotions to the point of violence.

As voluntary organizations have come to reflect more comprehensively the whole gamut of minority views and interests in society, so have they increased the strains placed on the reconciling function of the system of government. There thus develops the phenomenon that is often called the "new factionalism"; whatever position is proposed on some issue, by some group, it is opposed by an equally well-organized, articulate, lobby, pressure group, or voluntary organization. The government may satisfy one group but only at the cost of antagonizing another until all possibilities of movement are inhibited. In practice, the organizers of each group have a vested interest in not being satisfied, since once the group's demands have been met, their reason for existence would disappear.

The new factionalism not only arises because a wider spectrum has come to be represented by voluntary organizations. It can also be attributed to the way the basis of organization has changed. The traditional voluntary organizations — those that were important to politics in the past — were organized around a whole range of interests possessed by some particular class, ethnic, religious, or occupational group. Today many voluntary organizations are organized around a particular position on a political issue. Compared to the traditional interest groups, single-issue pressure groups have probably served to bring into the political process people for whom the old class and ethnic interests were no longer salient. However, the old class- and ethnic-based politics was more easily negotiated than are the newer, issue-based politics. There was more scope for wheeling and dealing between interest groups of the old traditional kind than there is between pressure groups each representing a single and often conflicting position on some particular issue. Whereas groups representing, say, management and labor can each give a bit and take a bit, it is difficult to see how two groups, one of which advocates nuclear power as the energy source of the future and the other committed to banning all nuclear power stations, can ever reach much accommodation. Fortunately, there are some signs that the Third Sector is beginning to develop organizations designed to introduce the negotiating mode into environmental disputes. A case in point would be the California-based RESOLVE Center for Environmental Conflict Resolution.

The concept of democracy that has been traditional in the West and to which I have frequently referred as "a free society" depends on both participation — as expressed in the time-honored phrase "government by consent of the governed" — and tolerance. Judge Learned Hand once wrote, "The spirit of liberty is the spirit which is not too sure that it is right."[3] In the language of Dahl's analysis, we might paraphrase this by saying that our concept of democracy depends on citizens recognizing, much of the time, that their policy preferences are weak. Voluntary organizations have done a good job in increasing participation. They have still to learn how to increase tolerance.

The argument discussed in this book does help us to understand why what we call a free society retains a range of institutions that are neither governmental nor commercial and thus gives us only a partial answer to the question with which we started. If we imagine a society that is solely dependent on market mechanisms, it would be an inadequate form of society lacking any adequate means of collective defense and lacking many of the amenities of civilized social existence. More significant, we cannot really imagine commerce without government. Market mechanisms ultimately depend on the concept of private property and contract, both of which derive from the law and thus depend on the existence of the three branches of government: a legislature to define the law, a judiciary to interpret it, and an executive to enforce it.

Economists have long been aware of the inherent limits of the market and welfare economics. In particular, in the theories of market failure and the like they have sought to define the theoretical limits on market operations. The attempt is not wholly successful, and the corresponding task of defining theoretical limits on government operations is even more difficult. The difficulty in the latter task springs in large part from the fact that what we call a free society, the way the idea of democracy is developed in the Western world, contains two different strands; one emphasizing the individual and hence diversity and one emphasizing the collectivity and hence uniformity. Only in an absolutely homogeneous society of which every member had the same desires and aspirations would there be no tension between these two strands and an unambiguous measure of social benefit. The institutions of the Third Sector are one of the principal sources of the flexibility that enables a free society to preserve both strands. They thus avoid both the practical injustices and the logical contradictions that would flow from the hard dichotomy of relying too heavily on either self-regarding market forces or an all-embracing role for government.

The argument that we might call the "twin failures argument" begins to provide a rationale for the Third Sector. I am conscious that much more could be done to develop the argument. In particular, I am aware that much more than I have attempted here needs to be done to identify the theoretical limits on the instrumentalities of government. Moreover, even if the argument were to be fully developed, there would still remain many questions to answer. How, for example, can we adequately explain the motivation for altruistic behavior? Is altruistic behavior a necessary ingredient in social life? How can altruistic behavior be encouraged? In this book I have drawn principally on the disciplines of economics and political theory and thus can only hope to provide a partial rationale for the Third Sector. A full rationale would need to draw on many other disciplines such as, for example, moral philosophy and the theories of justice, psychology, sociology, history, and so on. The systematic study of the Third Sector has only just begun. It has still a long way to go before it can command a set of concepts and analytic tools that can compare with those of economics or political science and before it can hope to rank as a discipline in its own right. Yet the endeavor to build up such a discipline is, I believe, worthwhile not only for its own sake but also for the light it will cast on other aspects of how humans live in society.

Notes

Chapter 1

1. *Giving in America.* Report of the Commission on Private Philanthropy and Public Need.

2. In spite of this, I do not intend in this book to distinguish sharply between these terms and propose to use terms "voluntary," "nonprofit," and "philanthropic," and "charitable" fairly loosely to describe different aspects of the Third Sector. The term "charitable," however, I will use in its legal sense, which has a somewhat different and in some respects rather wider meaning than it bears in common parlance.

3. Both the Patman hearings and their various sequels will be found discussed in Heimann, *The Future of Foundations.*

4. Weisbrod and Long, "The Size of the Voluntary Non-Profit Sector: Concepts and Measures," in Weisbrod, *The Voluntary Non-Profit Sector.*

5. Fremont-Smith, *Foundations and Government,* ch. 1.

6. The belief that a rationale of this sort must exist somewhere, if we could only locate it, is implicit in the essay I wrote with Aaron Wildavsky *(The Future of Foundations).*

7. Although in common parlance we distinguish charity from the functions of government, the legal definition of charity would include activities of a kind that are undertaken by government if only because lessening the burdens on government forms part of the definition of charity in both English and American law.

8. Hirschman, *The Passions and the Interests.*

9. "The Role of Non-Profit Enterprise." Discussed at greater length in Chapter 6.

10. Weisbrod, "Towards a Theory of the Non-Profit Sector." Discussed at greater length in Chapter 7.

Chapter 2

1. Lindblom, *Politics and Markets*, p. 17.
2. Dahl and Lindblom, *Politics, Economics and Welfare*, p. 106.
3. Lindblom, *Politics and Markets*, p. 17.
4. Rapoport, *N-Person Game Theory*.

Chapter 3

1. Edgeworth, *Mathematical Physics*.
2. Pareto, *Manuel d'Economie Politique*.
3. Allais, "Pareto, Vilfredo."
4. Pigou, *The Economics of Welfare;* Little, *A Critique of Welfare Economics;* Baumol, *Welfare Economics and the Theory of the State*.
5. Pigou, *The Economics of Welfare*, p. 183.
6. Wolf, *A Theory of Non-Market Failure*.
7. "Nous voyons donc maintenant que la consideration de l'état économique caracterisé par la libre concurrence des entrepreneurs, et la considération de l'état économique ou l'on obtient le maximum d'ophelimité pour la société, conduisent a des conditions identiques pour l'équilibre économique, non seulement de la production, mais aussi de la capitalisation, c'est-à-dire pour les conditions de l'équilibre économique en general." Pareto, *Cours d'Economie Politique*, p. 96, Sec. 725.
8. Alchian, *Pricing and Society*.
9. Robbins, *The Theory of Political Economy in English Political Economy*, p. 56.
10. Arrow, "Gifts and Exchanges," p. 24.
11. Bator, "The Anatomy of Market Failure."
12. See in particular Ronald Coase, "The Problem of Social Cost" and the works of Oliver E. Williamson quoted in the Bibliography. The illustration I give in the following paragraphs is taken principally from Williamson, "The Economics of Organization."
13. Samuelson, "The Pure Theory of Public Expenditures," p. 387.
14. Calabresi and Bobitt, *Tragic Choices*.
15. Weisbrod, "Towards a Theory of the Voluntary Non-Profit Sector."
16. Rose-Ackerman, "United Charities."
17. McKean, "Private Charity and Public Policy."

18. Nelson and Krashinsky, "Public Contract and Economic Organization of Day Care."

19. Hansmann, "The Role of Non-Profit Enterprise."

Chapter 4

1. *Restatement of the Law of Trusts*, Sect. 368.

2. *Halsbury's Law of England* (1979 Edition), Sect. 506.

3. Reg. 1.501 (C)(3)-1(d)(2) quoted Persons, Osborn, and Feldman, "Criteria for Exemption under Section 501 (c)(3)."

4. An even older list is to be found in the fourteenth-century poem *The Vision of Piers Plowman* by William Langland — "Repair hospitals, help sick people, mend bad roads, build up bridges that have broken down, help maidens to marry or to make them nuns, find food for prisoners or poor people, put scholars to school or some other craft, help religious orders and ameliorate rents and taxes."

5. See in particular the Appendix to the Goodman Committee Report.

6. Rose-Ackerman, "United Charities."

7. Picarda, *The Law and Practice Relating to Charities*, p. 32.

8. Wolf, *A Theory of Non-Market Failure*.

9. Bremmer, "Private Philanthropy and Public Needs: Historical Perspective," p. 99.

10. Calabresi, "Comment," pp. 57-61.

11. Sen, "Rational Fools."

12. The perfect altruist would be the man who saved the drowning child knowingly at the cost of his own life. This transaction defies conventional economic analysis, as we cannot put a price on either life. Few moral systems maintain that such heroic sacrifice is obligatory just as most would assert an obligation to save the child at trifling cost. Yet the moral judgments cannot be based on any form of economic calculus. We cannot say that we are relieved of the moral obligation to save the child's life when the cost to us exceeds a certain figure. Nor can we say that we are morally obliged to sacrifice our own life to save two children or ten or any other specific figure.

13. *Income Tax Special Commissioners v. Pemsel* (1891) A.C. 531.

14. See Chapter 6 for one theory why social clubs adopt the nonprofit form.

15. The English and the American legal systems are based on "common law." Most Western European legal systems are based on

legal codes (such as the Napoleonic Code) in which it is difficult to find the exact parallel to the law of charities. However, insofar as analogy can be made, there does seem to be in those systems also an antagonism between charitable and political objectives. See Pomey, *Traite Des Foundations d'Utilité Publique*, particularly Annexes 9 and 11.

16. Picarda, *The Law and Practice Relating to Charities*.

17. Persons, Osborn, and Feldman, "Criteria for Exemption under Section 501(c)(3)."

18. *Annual Report of the Charity Commissioners for England and Wales*, for the year 1969, paragraph 8.

19. This argument is reviewed by John Simon, "Foundations and Public Controvery: An Affirmative View."

Chapter 5

1. James Fishkin has suggested to me that this concept plays for Adam Smith a role very similar to that which for John Rawls is played by the "original position" in his *Theory of Justice*.

2. Smith, *Theory of Moral Sentiments*, pp. 9-10. Some authors have argued that between writing *The Theory of Moral Sentiments* and writing the *Wealth of Nations*, Adam Smith changed his view of the nature of man. This theory is discussed and effectively disproved by the editors of the most recent edition of *The Theory of Moral Sentiments*. See the edition by Raphael and Macfie, "Introduction," pp. 20-25.

3. Olson, *The Logic of Collective Action*, p. 6.

4. Robert Cameron Mitchell, "National Environment Lobbies and the Apparent Illogic of Collective Action."

5. Arrow, "Gifts and Exchanges," p. 18.

6. Dawkins, *The Selfish Gene*.

7. Ardrey, *The Social Contract*, and Wynne-Edwards, *Animal Dispersion in Relation to Social Behaviour*.

8. *The Selfish Gene*, p. 8. One way in which Dawkins's theory differs from that of the theologians is that "memes" may be morally good or bad, selfish or altruistic, whereas there is no countervailing power to "grace" except "fallen nature" itself.

9. Contained in the 12th Chapter of the First Letter to the Corinthians.

10. Quotations from the Ronald Knox translation of St. Paul's Epistles.

11. Wilks, *The Problem of Sovereignty in the Later Middle Ages*, pp. 23-25.

12. The illustration is drawn from the Goodman Committee Report, paragraph 27.

13. Quoted in Persons et al., "Criteria for Exemption Under Section 501(c)(3)."

14. For a much more comprehensive critique of the attempt to extend economics into the field of political decision-making by means of the techniques of cost-benefit analysis, see Self, *Econocrats and the Policy Process*.

15. Niskamen, *Bureaucracy and Representative Government*.

16. Weisbrod, "Towards a Theory of the Non-Profit Sector," p. 181.

17. See Jewkes and Jewkes, *Value for Money in Medicine*.

Chapter 6

1. 56 and 57 Vic Chap. 71, Section 14.

2. Geddling v. Marsh (1920) 1 KB 688.

3. Godley v. Perry (1960) 1 11 ER 36.

4. ,In practice the safeguards provided by the Sale of Goods Act are not wholly satisfactory because of the costs and complications of a procedure based on a civil action. More recent legislators in the United Kingdom as in the United States have tended to prefer the use of the criminal law. Nonetheless, as a theoretical statement of the principles involved, the two propositions — that the dealer is responsible for ensuring that the goods in which he or she trades are of merchantable quality and that the buyer should be able to rely on the skill and judgment of the seller that the goods are fit for their purpose — state very clearly the conditions required in commercial transactions.

5. For a recent review of this general position and alternative arguments, see a recent paper prepared for delivery at the 1979 Annual Meeting of the American Political Science Association by Jeffrey Obler, "Private Giving in the Welfare State."

6. Arrow, "Gifts and Exchanges," p. 22.

7. Nelson and Krashinsky, "Public Contract and Economic Organization of Day Care," p. 66.

8. Hansmann, "The Role of Non-Profit Enterprise."

9. Ellman, "On Developing a Law of Non Profit Corporations."
10. Hansmann, "The Role of Non-Profit Enterprise," p. 843.
11. Ibid., p. 847.
12. Ibid., p. 859.
13. Ibid., p. 861.
14. Ellman, "On Developing a Law of Non-Profit Corporations," p. 157.

Chapter 7

1. Tocqueville, *Democracy in America*, Part 2, Second Book, Chapter 5, p. 485.
2. Ibid.
3. Ibid.
4. Mavity and Ylvisaker, "Private Philanthropy and Public Affairs," p. 798.
5. Weisbrod, "Towards a Theory of the Non-Profit Sector," p. 172.
6. Friedman, *Capitalism and Freedom*, p. 15.
7. The Nathan Committee of 1952.

Chapter 8

1. Crossman, "Who Has the Last Word?" quoted in Lazar, "British Populism," p. 266.
2. Condorcet, *Essai sur l'Application de l'Analyse à la Probabilité des Decisions Rendues à la Pluralité des Voix*. Circular preferences are discussed with charming anecdotes of its exploitation by "Lewis Carroll" in Duncan Black's *The Theory of Committees and Elections*.
3. The way in which political institutions determine the order in which decisions are taken or "set the agenda" has been particularly studied by William Riker. See Bibliography.
4. Arrow's Impossibility Theorem or Paradox of Social Choice was originally developed by Arrow in *Social Choice and Individual Values* (1951). He has subsequently restated it in slightly different forms. The theorem is the subject of an unusually lucid study by MacKay: *Arrow's Theorem: The Paradox of Social Choice*, on whose formulation of it this summary is based. The theorem has been criticized notably by Sen,

Collective Choice and Social Welfare. But Sen and other critics, although they may reach their conclusion by somewhat different routes, also maintain the impossibility of aggregating preferences without making interpersonal judgments of welfare or otherwise restricting the type of preferences to be aggregated.

5. MacKay, *Arrow's Theorem*, pp. 5-6.

6. Riker, "Implications from the Disequilibrium of Majority Rule," p. 443.

7. Dahl, *A Preface to Democratic Theory*, pp. 90-103. I hope this redefinition of the case, without doing too much violence to Dahl's theory, will help to meet James Fishkin's objections to that case (see *Tyranny and Legitimacy*, pp. 12-16).

8. A study of a contemporary case in which these conditions apply, that of Ulster, is to be found in Rose, *Governing without Consensus*. The trouble spots of the world — Cyprus, Lebanon, Vietnam, and elsewhere — will offer several other illustrations of this case.

9. Dahl, *A Preface to Democratic Theory*, p. 133.

10. Burns, *The Deadlock of Democracy*.

11. A religion could encounter an intense belief on the part of the majority of citizens that it was bad. The English law is more discriminating in applying charitable status to religions than, despite Jonestown, is the American law derived from the First Amendment.

12. There are two other rationales for the tax deductibility of charitable contributions seen from the point of view of the taxpayer. First, the charitable contribution can be seen not as part of the income — as properly defined — of the donor but as part of the income of the donee, and since the donee is tax exempt, the contribution should not bear tax. This is manifestly the basis of the British system, but the argument can also be applied to the American tax. See William D. Andrews, "Personal Deductions in an Ideal Income Tax," pp. 2163-2219. Second, the state may recognize a duty to charity on the part of the taxpayer somewhat analogous to his responsibilities to his family so that the charitable deduction would be analogous to the individual exemptions for spouses, children, and so on. This would be another example of the way charities have something in common with families.

13. Brittan, "The Economic Contradictions of Democracy."

14. Schumpeter, *Capitalism, Socialism and Democracy*, ch. 7 and 8.

15. Kuznets and Jenks, *Capital in the American Economy*, p. 47.

16. This is a theme Aaron Wildavsky and I have developed elsewhere.

17. For a review of independent public policy research in the United

States, Britain and Canada, see Marsh, "Independent Public Policy Research."

18. Wolfenden Committee Report, pp. 41-43.

19. Sarason et al., *Human Services and Resource Networks.*

Chapter 9

1. Charities, since public benefit is necessary to the definition of a charitable purpose, must be concerned with objectives of social value. As discussed in Chapter 4 not all private nonprofit organizations concerned with objectives of social value are charities. Political parties and other private nonprofits with political objectives are not charities, but the pluralistic argument just summarized clearly applies to them no less than to charities.

2. I hope that Michael Krashinsky, to whom I owe this suggestion, will on some future occasion develop the argument for regarding the nonprofit form as a means of reducing transaction costs.

3. Judge Hand, *The Spirit of Liberty,* p. 190. Irving Dilliard in his "Introduction" to this volume tells us that Judge Hand was much impressed by Oliver Cromwell's plea before the Battle of Dunbar, "I beseech ye in the bowels of Christ, think that ye may be mistaken." The thought is similar.

Bibliography

ALCHIAN, A. A. (1967) Pricing and Society. London: Institute of Economic Affairs.

ALLAIS, M. (1968) "Pareto, Vilfredo: contributions to economics," p. 104 in International Encyclopedia of the Social Sciences, Vol. 2. New York: Macmillan.

ANDREWS, W. D. (1975) "Personal deductions in an ideal income tax," pp. 2163-2219 in Research Papers, Vol. 4. Sponsored by the Commission on Private Philanthropy and Public Need (Department of the Treasury). Washington, DC: Commission on Private Philanthropy and Public Need.

ARDREY, R. (1970) The Social Contract. London: Collins

ARROW, K. (1975) "Gifts and exchanges," in Edmund S. Phelps (ed.) Altruism, Morality and Economic Theory." New York: Russell Sage.

——— (1963) Social Choice and Individual Values. New Haven, CT: Yale University Press.

BATOR, F. M. (1958) "The anatomy of market failure." Quarterly Journal of Economics 72: 351-379.

BAUMOL, W. J. (1952) Welfare Economics and the Theory of the State. Cambridge, MA: Harvard University Press.

BERGER, P. L. and R. L. NEUHAUS (1977) To Empower People. Washington, DC: American Enterprise Institute.

BELL, D. (1973) The Coming of Post-Industrial Society. New York: Basic Books.

BLACK, D. (1958) The Theory of Committees and Elections. Cambridge: Cambridge University Press.

BRITTAN, S. (1975) "The economic contradictions of democracy." British Journal of Political Science 5: 129-159.

BREMMER, R. H. (1975) "Private philanthropy and public needs: historical perspective," pp. 89-114 in Research Papers, Vol. 1, Part II. Sponsored by the Commission on Private Philanthropy and Public Need (Department of the Treasury). Washington, DC: Commission on Private Philanthropy and Public Need.

BURNS, J. M. (1963) The Deadlock of Democracy. Englewood Cliffs, NJ: Prentice-Hall.

CALABRESI, G. (1975) "Comment," in Edmund S. Phelps (ed.) Altruism, Morality and Economic Theory. New York: Russell Sage.

——— and P. BOBBITT (1979) Tragic Choices. New York: W. W. Norton.

COASE, R. (1968) "The problem of social cost," in W. Brett and Harold Hochman (eds.) Readings in Micro-economics. New York: Holt, Rinehart & Winston.

CONDORCET, M. de (1972) 1875 Essai sur l'Application de l'analyse à la Probabilité des Decisions Rendues à la Majorite des Voix. New York: Chelsea.

CROSSMAN, R.H.S. (1970) "Who has the last word?" New Statesman (August 7). Quoted in H. Lazer, "British populism." Political Science Quarterly 91, 2 (1976).

DAHL, R. A. (1956) A Preface to Democratic Theory. Chicago: University of Chicago Press.

——— and C. E. LINDBLOM (1953) Politics, Economics and Welfare. New York: Harper.

DAWKINS, R. (1976) The Selfish Gene. Oxford: Oxford University Press.

EDGEWORTH, F. Y. (1967) [1881] Mathematical Physics: An Essay on the Application of Mathematics to the Moral Sciences. New York: A. M. Kelley.

ELLMAN, I. M. (1979) "On developing a law of non-profit corporations." Arizona State Law Journal, pp. 153-164.

FISHKIN, J. (1979) Tyranny and Legitimacy. Baltimore: Johns Hopkins University Press.

FREMONT-SMITH, M. R. (1975) Foundations and Government. New York: Russell Sage.

FRIEDMAN, M. (1962) Capitalism and Freedom. Chicago: University of Chicago Press.

Giving in America (1975) Report of the Commission on Private Philanthropy and Public Need. John H. Filer, Chairman. Washington, DC: Commission on Private Philanthropy and Public Need.

Goodman Committee (1976) Charity Law and Voluntary Organizations. Report of an independent committee of inquiry set up by the National Council of Social Service under the Chairmanship of Lord Goodman. London: Bedford Square.

HAND, L. (1954) The Spirit of Liberty. New York: Alfred K. Knopf.

HANSMANN, H.B. (1980) "Role of non-profit enterprise." Yale Law Journal 89 (April): 835-901.

HARDIN, G.J. and J. BADEN (1977) Managing the Commons. San Francisco: W. H. Freeman.

HEIMANN, F. [ed.] (1973) The Future of Foundations. Englewood Cliffs, NJ: Prentice-Hall.

HIRSCHMAN, A. O. (1973) The Passions and the Interests. Princeton, NJ: Princeton University Press.

——— (1970) Exit, Voice and Loyalty. Cambridge, MA: Harvard University Press.

JEWKES, J. and S. JEWKES (1963) Value for Money in Medicine. Oxford: Basil Blackwell.

KANT, I. (1949) Critique of Practical Reason (trans. and ed., Lewis White Beck). Chicago: University of Chicago Press.

KUZNETS, S. and E. JENKS (1961) Capital in the American Economy. Princeton, NJ: Princeton University Press.

KNOX, R. [trans.] (1956) The New Testament. New York: Sheed and Ward.

LINDBLOM, C.E. (1977) Politics and Markets. New York: Basic Books.

LITTLE, I.M.D. (1950) A Critique of Welfare Economics. Oxford: Clarendon.

MacKAY, A. (1980) Arrow's Theorem: The Paradox of Social Choice. New Haven, CT: Yale University Press.

MARSH, I. (1979) "Independent public policy research." (mimeo)

MAVITY, J. and P. YLVISAKER (1975) "Private philanthropy and public affairs," pp. 795-836 in Research Papers, Vol. 2. Sponsored by the Commission on Private Philanthropy and Public Need (Department of the Treasury). Washington, DC: Commission on Private Philanthropy and Public Need.

McKEAN, R. M. (1979) "Private charity and public policy." Paper presented to the Liberty Fund seminar, April, Miami.

MEAD, J. (1952) "External economies and diseconomies in a competitive situation." Economic Journal 62 (March): 54-67.

MITCHELL, R. C. (1979) "National environment lobbies and the apparent illogic of collective action," in Collective Decision-Making. Baltimore: Johns Hopkins University Press.

MULLIN, R. (1980) Present Alms. Birmingham: Phlogiston.

NASON, J.W. (1977) Trustees and the Future of Foundations. New York: Council on Foundations.

Nathan Committee (1952) Report of the Committee on the Law and Practice Relating to Charitable Trusts. Lord Nathan, Chairman. London: HMSO Cmd 8710.

NELSON, R. and M. KRASHINSKY (1974) "Public contract and economic organization of day care." Public Policy 22, 1: 53-75.

NEUHOFF, K. and U. PAVEL [eds.] (1971) Trusts and Foundations in Europe. London: Bedford Square.

NISKAMEN, W. A., Jr. (1971) Bureaucracy and Representative Government. Chicago: Aldine-Atherton.

OBLER, J. (1979) "Private giving and the welfare state." Paper presented at the Annual Meeting of the American Political Science Association.

OLSON, M. (1965) The Logic of Collective Action. Cambridge, MA: Harvard University Press.

OWEN, D. (1964) English Philanthropy 1660-1960. Cambridge, MA: Harvard University Press.

PARETO, V. (1971) [1906] Manuel d'Economie Politique (trans., Ann S. Schwyer). New York: A. M. Kelley.

——— (1964) Cours d'Economie Politique (ed., Bousquet and Busino). Geneva: Librairie Droz.

PERSONS, J. P., J.J. OSBORN, Jr., and C. F. FELDMAN (1975) "Criteria for exemption under Section 501 (c)(3)," pp. 1909-2044 in Research Papers, Vol. 4. Sponsored by the Commission on Private Philanthropy and Public Need (Department of the Treasury.) Washington, DC: Commission on Private Philanthropy and Public Need.

PHELPS, E. S. [ed.] (1975) Altruism, Morality and Economic Theory. New York: Russell Sage.

PICARDA, J. (1977) The Law and Practice Relating to Charities. London: Butterworth.

PIGOU, A.C. (1948) [1920] The Economics of Welfare. London: Macmillan.

POMEY, M. (1980) Traite des Foundations d'Utilité Publique. Presse Universitaire de France.

RAPOPORT, A. (1970) N-Person Game Theory. Ann Arbor: University of Michigan Press.

RAWLS, J. (1971) A Theory of Justice. Cambridge, MA: Belknap.
Restatement of the Law of Trusts (1959) American Law Institute.
Riker, W. H. (1982) Liberalism Against Populism: A Confrontation Between the Theory of Democracy and the Theory of Social Choice. San Francisco: H. W. Freeman.
——— (1980) "Implications from the disequilibrium of majority rule." American Political Science Review 74: 432-446.
——— (1961) "Voting and the summation of preferences." American Political Science Review 55: 990-911.
——— (1958) "The paradox of voting and congressional rules for voting on amendments." American Political Science Review 52: 349-367.
ROBBINS, L. (1952) The Theory of Political Economy in English Political Economy. London Macmillan.
ROSE, R. (1971) Governing Without Consensus. London: Faber.
ROSE-ACKERMAN, S. (1980) "United Charities: an economic analysis." Public Policy 28 (Summer): 323-350.
ROWE, A. (1975) Democracy Renewed. London: Sheldon.
SAMUELSON, P. A. (1954) "The pure theory of public expenditures." Review of Economics and Statistics 36: 387-389.
SARASON, S. B., C. CARROLL, K. MATON, S. COHEN, and E. LORENTZ (1977) Human Services and Resource Networks. San Francisco: Jossey-Bass.
SELF, P. J. O. (1977) Econocrats and the Policy Process. Boulder, CO: Westview.
SCHUMPETER, J. A. (1976) Capitalism, Socialism and Democracy. London: Allen & Unwin.
SEN, A. K. (1977) "Rational fools: a critique of the behavioural foundations of economic theory." Philosophy and Public Affairs 6, 4.
——— (1970) Collective Choice and Social Welfare. San Francisco: Holden Day.
SIMON, J. G. (1978) "Charity and dynasty." The Probate Lawyer. New York: American College of Probate Counsel.
SMITH, A. (1976) The Theory of Moral Sentiments (eds., D. D. Raphael and A. L. Macfie). Oxford: Clarendon.
——— An Inquiry into the Nature and Causes of the Wealth of Nations (eds., R. H. Campbell and A. S. Siknner). Oxford: Clarendon.
TITMUSS, R. (1971) The Gift Relationship. New York: Pantheon.
TOCQUEVILLE, A. de (1974) Democracy in America (trans., Henry Reeve). New York: Schocken.
WEISBROD, B. A. [ed.] (1977) The Voluntary Non-Profit Sector. Lexington, MA: D. C. Heath.

——— (1975) "Towards a theory of the non-profit sector," in Edmund S. Phelps (ed.) Altruism, Morality and Economic Theory. New York: Russell Sage.

WILDAVSKY, A. and J. DOUGLAS (1978) The Future of Foundations. New Rochelle, NY: Change Magazine.

WILKS, M. (1963) The Problem of Sovereignty in the Later Middle Ages. Cambridge: Cambridge University Press.

WILLIAMSON, P.E. (1981) "The economics of organization: the transaction cost approach." American Journal of Sociology 87, 3.

——— (1979) "Transaction cost economics: the governance of contractual relations." Journal of Law and Economics 22: 233-261.

——— (1973) "Markets and hierarchies: some elementary considerations." American Economics Association. Organizational Forms and Internal Efficiency 63, 2.

WOLF, C., Jr. (1978) A Theory of Non-Market Failure. Santa Monica, CA: Rand P 60234.

Wolfenden Committee Report (1978) The Future of Voluntary Organizations. London: Croom Helm.

WYNNE-EDWARDS, V.C. (1962) Animal Dispersion in Relation to Social Behaviour. Edinburgh: Oliver & Boyd.

YOUNG, D.R. and W.E. MOORE (1964) Trusteeship and the Management of Foundations. New York: Russell Sage.

ZURCHER, A.J. and J. DUSTAN (1972) The Foundation Administrator. New York: Russell Sage.

Index

About the Author

JAMES DOUGLAS was affiliated with Britain's Conservative (Party) Research Department for more than two decades, most recently as Director (1970-1974) and as Consultant Director (1974-1977). Both during that period and since, he has held visiting appointments at the University of Illinois, the Russell Sage Foundation, and at Yale, Princeton, and Columbia Universities. Since 1981, he has been Adjunct Associate Professor of Political Science and Public Management at Northwestern University. He wrote (with Aaron Wildavsky) *The Future of Foundations: Some Reconsiderations* (Change Magazine Press, 1978). He was one of the founders of the British Consumers' Association and currently serves as its Honorary Vice President. Professor Douglas was awarded the O.B.E. in 1959 for his service to British politics.